TELL YOUR HEART to BEAT AGAIN

DUTCH SHEETS

TELL YOUR HEART
to BEAT
AGAIN

DUTCH
SHEETS

Regal

From Gospel Light
Ventura, California, U.S.A.

Published by Regal Books
From Gospel Light
Ventura, California, U.S.A.
Printed in the U.S.A.

Regal Books is a ministry of Gospel Light, an evangelical Christian
publisher dedicated to serving the local church. We believe God's vision
for Gospel Light is to provide church leaders with biblical,
user-friendly materials that will help them evangelize, disciple and
minister to children, youth and families.

It is our prayer that this Regal book will help you discover
biblical truth for your own life and help you meet the needs of
others. May God richly bless you.

*For a free catalog of resources from Regal Books/Gospel Light, please call your
Christian supplier or contact us at* 1-800-4-GOSPEL *or* www.regalbooks.com.

Rights for publishing this book in other languages are contracted by
Gospel Light Worldwide, the international nonprofit ministry of
Gospel Light. Gospel Light Worldwide also provides publishing and
technical assistance to international publishers dedicated to producing
Sunday School and Vacation Bible School curricula and books in the
languages of the world. For additional information,
visit www.gospellightworldwide.org;
write to Gospel Light Worldwide, P.O. Box 3875, Ventura, CA 93006; or
send an e-mail to info@gospellightworldwide.org.

All Scripture quotations, unless otherwise indicated, are taken from the *New American Standard Bible,* © 1960, 1962, 1963, 1968, 1971, 1972, 1973, 1975, 1977 by The Lockman Foundation. Used by permission.

Other versions used are
AMP—Scripture taken from *THE AMPLIFIED BIBLE*, Old Testament copyright © 1965, 1987 by the Zondervan Corporation. The Amplified New Testament copyright © 1958, 1987 by The Lockman Foundation. Used by permission.
KJV—*King James Version.* Authorized King James Version.
THE MESSAGE—Scripture taken from *THE MESSAGE.* Copyright © by Eugene H. Peterson, 1993, 1994, 1995. Used by permission of NavPress Publishing Group.
Moffatt—*The Bible: James Moffatt Translation* by James A. R. Moffatt. Copyright © 1922, 1924, 1925, 1926, 1935 by Harper Collins San Francisco. Copyright 1950, 1952, 1953, 1954 by James A. R. Moffatt.
NIV—Scripture taken from the *Holy Bible, New International Version*®. Copyright © 1973, 1978, 1984 by International Bible Society. Used by permission of Zondervan Publishing House. All rights reserved.
TLB—Scripture quotations marked (*TLB*) are taken from *The Living Bible,* copyright © 1971. Used by permission of Tyndale House Publishers, Inc., Wheaton, IL 60189. All rights reserved.

Cover and interior design by Robert Williams

Library of Congress Cataloging-in-Publication Data
Sheets, Dutch.
    Tell your heart to beat again / Dutch Sheets.
        p. cm.
Includes bibliographical references.
    ISBN 0-8307-3078-8 (hardcover)   0-8307-3070-2 (paperback)
Hope—Religious aspects—Christianity.   I. Title.
    BV4638 .S44 2002
    234'.25—dc21   2002006542

1 2 3 4 5 6 7 8 9 / 09 08 07 06 05 04 03 02

CONTENTS

TRADING SORROW FOR JOY

The following is a testimony from my secretary. Although her story is different from yours or mine, her hope deferred has a familiar resonance for anyone who has ever experienced pain, disillusionment and loss of hope. Think of her story as a template, if you will, for how God can rise upon your darkness and deliver you into the glorious light of His presence to a hope-filled life. —DS

On January 11, 2002, author and speaker Chuck Pierce spoke at our church. That night, while he was ministering, the Lord suddenly quickened in my heart that it was exactly seven years—to the minute—since my daughter had told me the devastating details about my ex-husband's immoral and reprehensible activities. I was totally caught off guard by this memory; but as I thought about it and reviewed the events that had taken place years ago, I realized it was indeed the anniversary of that significant day.

God then continued to speak other things to me during that service, including, "Seven symbolizes completion—ending. The turmoil, despair and hopelessness of these past years are coming to an end. You are coming into the fullness of your healing. It's almost finished. I want you to know that this year you are going to be whole. Hope, joy and life are coming to you very soon. You will be victorious over hope deferred. This will be a year of new beginnings."

I was greatly encouraged by this and other things the Lord ministered to me that weekend, and I recognized an expectancy—even a hope—inside of me. During the next few weeks I sensed a greater level of faith, especially while I meditated in the Word. But then the realities and stresses of life began to overwhelm me once again. I got so busy that I forgot what the Lord had just ministered to me.

In the midst of this, Pastor Dutch, who had been scheduled to write a book about synergy, then decided to instead write about hope deferred. As I typed his manuscript, sometimes I could hardly see my computer screen through the tears. So much of what he had written, I had lived. But why was I still struggling? How could I still be at this horrible place of hope deferred? I had heard him teach on this, I had tried to follow these steps to healing, and now I was even working for him as he wrote about it. Yet I still hadn't experienced freedom in this area. Why? The frustration, shame, despair and struggle to believe were almost more than I could endure.

February 2002 seemed to be filled with horrible times of hope deferred. I couldn't understand it, but my emotional state seemed worse instead of better. At times I felt as though hope didn't exist at all—hopelessness seemed to pervade my entire life, no matter how much I reminded myself of how blessed I truly was. I didn't want to be in that place of despair, and I tried to fight my way out of it, but I just couldn't find any hope.

Then as I typed his manuscript, I came to what Pastor Dutch wrote about Abraham, quoting from Romans 4:18: "In hope against hope he believed." I determined to do the same—to hope whether I had any hope or not. That phrase came to my mind often during the next days, and I told myself, "You're going to hope whether you have hope or not!" Another thing that really struck me was Pastor Dutch's challenge to apply praise and worship as therapy. Although I had been meditating on Scripture, I had been focused on myself. I realized I needed to focus on praising and worshiping the Lord in my battle against hope deferred. I began to do so.

February 28 should have been a wonderful day of celebration in my life. My second granddaughter was born. As I held her just minutes after her birth, I marveled at the amazing wonders of our Creator God. Yet, at the same time, I struggled to hold back the tears. Somehow, the weight and grief of single parenting—even single grandparenting—just seemed too much to bear. Even as I left the hospital room, it was all I could do to keep from sobbing out loud as I tried to wipe away tears inconspicuously. As soon as I reached my van, I began to weep uncontrollably and continued to do so for hours after I got home, crying out to God to help me hope against hope and somehow be an overcomer.

The next day I struggled through work, fighting a terrible headache as a result of the hours of crying. Realizing that I could never make it through the special church service we had scheduled for that night unless I got some reprieve, I went home to rest. I remembered that praise and worship are a weapon against hope deferred, so I popped in a worship CD before I lay down. I tried to focus on worshiping God as I listened to the music and relaxed. Several minutes had gone by—probably about the fourth song on the CD—when suddenly the Lord began to speak to me:

> I'm going to heal you of hope deferred tonight. Tonight is seven weeks since Chuck ministered on January 11, when I told you your healing was almost finished. And tonight is also exactly seven years since the church body was told what your ex-husband had done. It is complete—finished. The devastation, despair, shame and hopelessness you have lived with will be gone. I am going to heal you and bring you into a place of new beginnings. Hope deferred will be broken off of you tonight, and hope, joy and peace will be restored to you. Your life will never be the same.

Well, being the woman of great faith that I am, I crawled out of bed and stumbled to look at a calendar, thinking, *It can't be seven weeks since Chuck was here.* I counted from January 11 to March 1—exactly seven weeks. My eyes popped open. *Well, okay, but it couldn't possibly also be seven years to the day since the church body found out what my ex-husband had done.* I dug around to find some old records. Sure enough, March 1, 1995, exactly seven years ago, was when his sin had been rightfully exposed. (This was necessary because he had been an associate pastor, and his sin had involved minors in the church.)

My spirit began to revive within me as I was filled with expectancy of what God was going to do in my life that night. He was going to finish His work of healing. Wholeness and completeness were coming to me! I was going to be Joy—not just in name but in my very being.

As I walked into the sanctuary that night, the excitement in my spirit continued to grow. During the time of worship, suddenly it was as though this huge deposit of hope, joy and life just hit me and literally knocked me over. Pastor Sam Brassfield ministered that night and gave a powerful word of the Lord about revival. As he shared, he often referred to the number seven—to its being a time of completion and new beginnings!

As I reveled in the healing power of God, I also realized that the previous day—February 28—had been the seventh anniversary of the day my ex-husband left our family for good. No wonder I had been overwhelmed with grief and the load of single-parenting! But, oh, the wonderful mercy and grace of our Father God!

When I was growing up, my goal was to be a wife and mother. I had even planned my family. I had wanted to have seven children: two girls, a boy, twin girls, a boy and then another girl. And I had even decided how old I wanted to be when each of my babies would be born. The Lord was faithful to honor my desire—and I was incredibly and unbelievably blessed to have six children, including twin girls, in the order and at the times in my life I had wanted. What an amazing God! However, I never did have the seventh child.

Until I started my road to healing several years ago, I couldn't imagine articulating to anyone the real reason why I chose not to have a seventh child—potentially a fifth daughter. And I never shared with my family why I made this decision, based on the hopelessness in my life. I didn't want them to know how truly hope deferred I was. But because God has now healed me and given me hope, I am able to testify to His goodness and grace. You see, my four daughters have the following middle names: Joy, Faith, Grace and Charity. So I knew that if I had another daughter, her middle name would be Hope—but that was impossible. My life was so deluged with hope deferred that there was absolutely no way I could have a child with the name Hope. It would have been the ultimate lie. Thus I decided not to have a seventh child.

Remember that I said my granddaughter was born on February 28, 2002, the seventh anniversary of the day when hope deferred catapulted into high gear in my life? Want to take a guess at what my son and daughter-in-law decided to name their new baby, without having any idea of the significance this would have for me? Katlyn Hope Anderson! *But God!*

GET BUSY LIVIN'

IN 1965, DURING A FAMILY REUNION IN FLORIDA, A GRANDMOTHER WOKE EVERYONE AT 2:00 A.M., ISSUING ORDERS TO GET EMPTY COKE BOTTLES, CORKS AND PAPER. "I'VE RECEIVED A MESSAGE FROM GOD," SHE SAID. "PEOPLE MUST HEAR HIS WORD." SHE WROTE VERSES ON THE PAPER, WHILE THE GRANDCHILDREN BOTTLED AND CORKED THEM. THEN EVERYONE DEPOSITED OVER 200 BOTTLES INTO THE SURF AT COCOA BEACH.

PEOPLE CONTACTED AND THANKED HER FOR THE SCRIPTURES THROUGHOUT THE YEARS. SHE DIED IN NOVEMBER 1974. THE NEXT MONTH THE LAST LETTER ARRIVED:

Dear Mrs. Gause,

I'm writing this letter by candlelight. We no longer have electricity on the farm. My husband was killed in the fall when the tractor overturned. He left 11 young children and myself behind. The bank is foreclosing, there's one loaf of bread left, there's snow on the ground, and Christmas is two weeks away. I prayed for forgiveness before I went to drown myself. The river has been frozen over for weeks, so I didn't think it would take long. When I broke the ice, a Coke bottle floated up. I opened it, and with tears and trembling hands, I read about hope. Ecclesiastes 9:4 "But for him who is joined to all the living there is hope." Hebrews 7:19; 6:18; and John 3:3 were also referenced. I came home, read my Bible, and am thanking God. Please pray for us, but we're going to make it now.

May God bless you and yours.

—A farm in Ohio[1]

How did this life-saving Coke bottle get from Cocoa Beach, Florida, to a river in Ohio nine years later? Not just any river, mind you, but the *right* river, near the *right* farm, at the *right* time?

I can almost hear the "Mrs. Gause Coke Bottle Angel Patrol" heaving a sigh of relief when the last message of hope was delivered nine years after it had been sent. And I can almost hear God's explanation to the angels: "This last one will be a Christmas present, much like the first one I delivered to hopeless humans 2,000 years ago."

Coke bottles were transformed into hope bottles—three of the four verses in the bottle were about hope. Imagine that! Not about God's power, or miracles, or even provision, which this lady certainly needed desperately. No, those things come *after* hope.

> A great artist was once asked, "What's the best picture you've ever painted?"
>
> "The next one," he replied confidently.
>
> But another artist, though in the height of his glory, was heard to lament, "Too bad I failed."
>
> "Why do you say that?" asked a friend of his in astonishment.
>
> "Because I've lost any hope of improvement," he said. He was right. For the person who has stopped hoping, failure is inevitable.[2]

Hope is to life what seeds are to the earth. We can't be fruitful without it. Life is sterile without hope: Dreams can't be produced and destinies will not be fulfilled. Every good thing produced in life is born of hope. That's why God starts there. Even faith is "the substance of things *hoped* for" (Heb. 11:1, *KJV*, emphasis added). Someone once said, "Where there is no faith in the future, there is no power in the present."[3]

In the movie *The Shawshank Redemption,* Andy (played by Tim Robbins), and Red (played by Morgan Freeman) are both serving life sentences for murder.[4] Red was guilty; Andy wasn't. It's a movie about injustice, despair, friendship, hope—especially hope—and finally, vindication. In one scene, talking about the sustaining power of music, Andy explained that keeping music alive in the heart demonstrates "there's something inside they can't get to, they can't touch."

"What are you talking about?" Red asks.

"Hope."

Speaking from a perspective of having spent nearly 50 years in prison, Red says, "Hope is a dangerous thing. It can drive a man insane. It's got no use on the inside of prison. Better get used to that idea."

Later in the movie, speaking again of the hope of freedom, Andy sums it all up with one profound statement, "I guess it comes down to a simple choice, really: Get busy livin' or get busy dyin'."

Andy was right. To be without hope is to start the dying process—literally.

In 1997 the journal of the American Heart Association reported on some remarkable research. According to the *Chicago Tribune,* Susan Everson of the Human Population Laboratory of the Public Health Institute in Berkeley, California, found that people who experienced high levels of despair had a 20 percent greater occurrence of atherosclerosis— the narrowing of the arteries—than did optimistic people. "This is the same magnitude of increased risk that one sees in comparing a pack-a-day smoker to a non-smoker," said Everson. In other words, despair can be as bad for you as smoking a pack a day![5]

A recent *Reader's Digest* article reported that people with serious depression were three times more likely to die of heart disease; and even those with mild depression had a fatality rate 50 percent higher than normal.[6]

God told us that a long time ago. Proverbs 13:12 says, "Hope deferred makes the heart sick, but desire fulfilled is a tree of life." Of course, I know He was speaking of the spiritual heart, but it's true of both. Hope deferred creates diseased hearts, both physically and spiritually. And with a diseased heart a person can't run life's race effectively.

HOPE DEFERRED IS THE COMMON COLD OF THE SOUL, EXCEPT THAT THIS VIRUS CAN KILL.

"Let us run with endurance the race that is set before us," we are exhorted in Hebrews 12:1; but a lack of endurance is one of the first results of heart disease. "Run in such a way that you may win," the Lord urges us through Paul's words in 1 Corinthians 9:24. That's almost like saying, "Get busy livin'," isn't it? But when hope deferred sets in, not only are we unable to win—sometimes we can't even finish the race. The loss of hope is crippling, making us little more than spectators at best or, at worst, like the suicidal lady in our opening story who had lost the will to live.

I don't want the pain, frustration or disillusionment of hope deferred to affect my heart in any way. I want to run the race of life effectively. Don't you? And not only effectively but also enthusiastically and with pleasure, enjoying the journey. And most certainly, the Lord wants this for us too.

No one makes it through life without suffering hope deferred to one degree or another. It's the common cold of the soul, except that this virus can kill. The symptoms appear to various degrees and in different forms, ranging from discouragement to depression, doubt to cynicism, and grief to suicidal tendencies. Hope deferred produces resignation, fear, unbelief, loss of passion, retreat from life and a host of other heart-disease maladies. It imprisons the soul.

King David, the great worshiping warrior of Israel, experienced it during the time when he was being falsely accused of disloyalty and he fled for his life and lived in caves. Listen to him battle hope deferred in Psalm 142:

> When my spirit was overwhelmed within me, Thou didst know my path. In the way where I walk they have hidden a trap for me. Look to the right and see; for there is no one who regards me; there is no escape for me; no one cares for my soul. *Bring my soul out of prison,* so that I may give thanks to Thy name (vv. 3-4,7, emphasis added).

Hope deferred had imprisoned David's soul. Three times in Psalms 42 and 43, also written from the cave, he had to command his soul to hope (see Pss. 42:5,11; 43:5). These verses are almost exactly the same, so quoting one of them is adequate: "Why are you in despair, O my soul? And why have you become disturbed within me? Hope in God, for I shall yet praise Him, the help of my countenance, and my God" (Ps. 42:11).

Don't let hope deferred imprison your soul. Get busy livin'. Be a "prisoner of hope" (Zech. 9:12, *AMP*).

Chris Jackson, one of my spiritual sons and my associate pastor, shared the following comments on hope's ability to release us from prison:

> Hosea addresses the staggering power of hope as he prophesies of the unquenchable love of God for His unfaithful people. He says in chapter 2, verse 15, "I will give her . . . the valley of Achor as a door of hope." The word *Achor* literally means "trouble." We can sense the great confidence of the Lord as He says, in essence, "I will give you, my weary and hurting people, a hope that opens doors in the midst of troublesome valleys." Hosea continues by saying that once hope opens a door "she will sing there as in the days of her youth" (2:15).
>
> What insight into the love of God and the power of hope! A word from God can spark enough hope to open a door of escape from our trouble. On the other side of that door is renewed youthfulness and a long-forgotten, unsung song of the Lord.

You may not feel like it, but, like Israel of old, you can rise above every disappointment by the power of the Holy Spirit. "Now may the God of hope fill you with all joy and peace in believing, that you may abound in hope *by the power of the Holy Spirit*" (Rom. 15:13, emphasis added).

Listen to one of my church members share about hope deferred in her life:

> The verse Romans 15:13 is underlined in my Bible, taped to my computer at work, written on a dog-eared piece of paper in my Day-Timer and has been a lifeline in my battle against hope deferred. I have read this verse nearly every day for the past few years, along with other Scriptures, as I have endeavored to apply the strategies Pastor Dutch has shared with our fellowship.
>
> My life has been filled with experiences that led to a life-threatening condition of hope deferred, including sexual abuse, my father's death when I was a child, years of a spouse's immoral actions, cancer, divorce—and that's just a partial list. In fact, when seeking professional help from a psychiatrist, he was kind enough to tell me that in all his years of practice he had only encountered a couple other life histories that were as devastating as mine. He also told me that I had lived under excessive stress for so many years that my mind had quit working properly, even comparing it to a heart that

eventually gives out from heart disease. His diagnosis was that I would probably never be able to function again normally. Thank God for pastors, friends and family who staked themselves to me and told me I would make it!

There were times when I didn't believe them—in fact, to be honest, a lot of times. Even though I have been privileged to sit under one of the best Bible teachers in the world, sometimes I felt like the principles weren't working in my life. And then the shame and condemnation would really set in. I had the keys and strategies right there in front of me. Why weren't they working? There must be something wrong with me. Sometimes I felt like such a failure that just to keep living was a tremendous struggle. I desperately wanted to run away from it all. I cannot count how many times, in the midst of feeling like hope did not exist, that I literally had to force myself just to tell myself to hope in God.

Now, I want you to know that these past years have also had times of victories and gaining ground over hope deferred. It has been an intense battle. But I can now confidently testify that the principles and strategies contained in this book do work. I have recently experienced an incredible healing in my life that is beyond anything I could have possibly imagined!

What causes this condition described by the Scriptures as hope deferred? It's really very simple—unfulfilled or shattered hopes and dreams, such as

- the death of a loved one;
- a failed marriage—or one that never occurred;
- the business that went under—you built it and they didn't come;
- the family member who still hasn't been saved;
- a promise unkept, betrayal, rejection or false accusation;
- a gallant fight of faith that was seemingly lost;
- as David experienced, false accusation, life in a cave and a seemingly lost destiny;
- as in Abraham's life, an Ishmael that God won't accept and an Isaac you can't produce.

The list is endless; but simply put, hope deferred is when the dream dies or when, if still there, it is laced with fear. If it now hurts when you think about the dream, you probably have hope deferred. If passion has waned and apathy has encroached, hope deferred is probably at work. If you find yourself going through the religious motions, doing and saying the right things while all the while feeling empty and lifeless on the inside, you may be a victim of this enemy.

If disappointment seems stronger than joy in your life; if tears come to your eyes when you think about a certain person; if you can't go to some places in your mind and heart without discomfort or negative emotion; if the promise now sparks disillusionment or cynicism instead of faith; if the statement "God is going to come through for you" is met with any doubt or questioning whatsoever; then you probably have some stage of heart disease.

Let me say from the start that experiencing the condition of hope deferred doesn't make you bad, weak or unspiritual; it makes you human. Consider the following U.S. statistics, all of which are linked to loss of hope. They're not pretty, but they are reality.

- The divorce rate has risen 279 percent in the last 27 years.7
- 2.5 million people in the U.S divorce each year (50 percent of first marriages and 60 percent of re-marriages).
- One million children are affected by new divorces each year.
- Fatherless homes account for 63 percent of youth suicides, 90 percent of homeless/runaway children and 85 percent of youths in prison.[8]
- Approximately 19 million adults have a depressive disorder, and the leading cause of disability is major depressive disorder.
- The youth suicide rate has tripled in the past 35 years, making suicide the third leading cause of death among 15- to 24-year-olds.[9]
- Approximately 25 percent of high school students

seriously consider suicide each year.[10]
- Psychiatric admissions account for 25 percent of total hospital admissions.[11]
- Even our spiritual leaders are not immune from this disease—70 percent of pastors constantly fight depression.
- 80 percent of adult children of pastors seek professional help for depression.
- 50 percent of pastors would leave the ministry if they could but have no other way to make a living.
- 1,500 pastors leave the ministry each month.[12]

Now for a piece of good news. I'm sure you're ready for some. Although it can be, hope deferred heart disease doesn't have to be fatal. There is a fail-proof antidote. Jesus, the great Physician, came "to heal the brokenhearted" (Luke 4:18, *KJV*), which is nothing more than an advanced stage of hope deferred. Listen to the words of Albert Edward Day:

> We have confidence that out of the very soil that is reddened by the blood of our broken hearts, there shall blossom life that is as endless as the life of God. Against all the demons of fear and despair that roam through the shadows of ignorance and skepticism Jesus sets His cross. There it stands today, the one sufficient bulwark of our hope, because it reveals to us a purpose and a power to resolve the tragedy into

transfiguration and to crown every tomb with the hope of a resurrection.[13]

With everything that is in me, I believe God wants to crown every tomb with a resurrection. Abraham and Sarah discovered this wonderful truth. Theirs was an extreme case of hope-deferred-induced heart disease. Hear them laughing cynically when after 24 years of waiting, God came to them one last time, promising Isaac. You may even recognize the laugh.

> Then Abraham fell on his face and laughed, and said in his heart, "Will a child be born to a man one hundred years old? And will Sarah, who is ninety years old, bear a child?" And Abraham said to God, "Oh that Ishmael might live before Thee!" (Gen. 17:17-18).

> And he said, "I will surely return to you at this time next year; and behold, Sarah your wife shall have a son." And Sarah was listening at the tent door, which was behind him. Now Abraham and Sarah were old, advanced in age; Sarah was past childbearing. And Sarah laughed to herself, saying, "After I have become old, shall I have pleasure, my lord being old also?" (Gen. 18:10-12).

Make no mistake about it, they were in trouble. Once cynicism hits, heart disease is in its advanced stage. Here is a likely progression of unchecked hope deferred:

1. Discouragement, the early stage of this disease
2. Confusion, wherein we begin to question ourselves, our dreams and God's promises
3. Unbelief, wherein hope is lost and expectation is gone
4. Disillusionment, the first stage of bitterness, which usually involves questioning even the character of God
5. Bitterness, wherein with deep feelings of resentment we blame God, others and maybe even ourselves
6. Cynicism, a complete loss of faith and hope—a dead heart

Abraham and Sarah experienced all of the above. Their faith for a child was dead; they were cynical. But don't stop there. Hear also God's final witness of a healed Abraham and Sarah who broke through to faith and fulfillment, just like you are going to do.

> In hope against hope he believed, in order that he might become a father of many nations, according to that which had been spoken, "So shall your descendants be" (Rom. 4:18).

> By faith even Sarah herself received ability to conceive, even beyond the proper time of life, since she

considered Him faithful who had promised (Heb. 11:11).

If Abraham and Sarah could move from such an extreme stage of hope deferred to strong, vibrant faith, so can you. "Hope against hope" is a powerful phrase. In the face of absolute hopelessness, Abraham hoped anyway!

How about Moses, the sick-hearted, unbelieving cynic who refused to believe that God could ever use him again? After all, 40 years of failure and isolation is a lot of hope deferred.

> But Moses said to God, "Who am I, that I should go to Pharaoh, and that I should bring the sons of Israel out of Egypt?" (Exod. 3:11).

> But he said, "Please, Lord, now send the message by whomever Thou wilt" [*in other words: "Not by me"*] (Exod. 4:13).

Moses was past believing. Any faith he had for fulfilling his destiny and helping his fellow Israelites had been dead for a long time. But the God who brings hope to the hopeless re-entered his life through a burning bush, opened up his clogged arteries, gave him a good shot of adrenaline and said, "Let's go, Moses. I'm not finished with you." And listen to Moses' victorious epitaph:

Since then no prophet has risen in Israel like Moses, whom the LORD knew face to face, for all the signs and wonders which the LORD sent him to perform in the land of Egypt against Pharaoh, all his servants, and all his land, and for all the mighty power and for all the great terror which Moses performed in the sight of all Israel (Deut. 34:10-12).

That qualifies as a bona fide overcomer of hope deferred!

I can't wait to tell you more about these and other overcomers of hope deferred—the Scriptures are filled with their stories. God is not only going to heal you, but He is also going to use this awful condition to make you a champion. But we're not quite there yet; for this chapter, the point is clear: Hope deferred and its resulting heart disease are not incurable.

In the *Pentecostal Evangel*, J.K. Gressett writes about a man named Samuel S. Scull, who settled on a farm in the Arizona desert with his wife and children:

> One night a fierce desert storm struck with rain, hail, and high wind. At daybreak, feeling sick and fearing what he might find, Samuel went to survey their loss.
>
> The hail had beaten the garden and truck patch into the ground; the house was partially unroofed; the henhouse had

blown away and dead chickens were scattered about. Destruction and devastation were everywhere.

While standing dazed, evaluating the mess and wondering about the future, he heard a stirring in the lumber pile that was the remains of the henhouse. A rooster was climbing up through the debris and he didn't stop climbing until he had mounted the highest board in the pile. That old rooster was dripping wet, and most of his feathers were blown away. But as the sun came over the eastern horizon, he flapped his bony wings and proudly crowed.[14]

When the morning sun appeared on the horizon amidst all the chaos and devastation, that beat-up, featherless rooster could still crow! Why? *Because it was his nature to crow.*

Winds of adversity may have blown through your life. Your world may be falling apart; but if you will look closely enough, you'll see the light of God's faithfulness shining through the debris. And you can rise above it because *it is your nature to overcome!* Listen to what God says about you in Romans 8:35-39, which is laced with hope:

Do you think anyone is going to be able to drive a wedge between us and Christ's love for us? There is no way. Not trouble, not hard times, not hatred, not hunger, not homelessness, not bullying threats, not backstabbing, not even the worst sins listed in Scripture. . . . None of this phases us because Jesus loves us. I'm absolutely convinced that nothing— nothing living or dead, angelic or demonic, today or tomorrow, high or low, thinkable or unthink- able—absolutely nothing can get between us and God's love because of the way that Jesus our Master has embraced us (*THE MESSAGE*).

Before God is finished, you're gonna climb up out of the debris. Your soul will be delivered from the prison of hope deferred so you can *get busy livin'*!

CHAPTER 2

Run with
Hope

WERNER LEMKE, WHO GREW UP IN GERMANY DURING WORLD WAR II, RELATES AN EXPERIENCE FROM THE WAR. THE ALLIED FORCES WERE AD-VANCING, AND HIS FAMILY HAD TO MOVE. WHEN THEY WERE READY TO LEAVE, THEY STOPPED TO TAKE A FINAL LOOK AT THEIR HOME. AN OLDER BROTHER SAID, "WAIT A MINUTE." GOING TO THE PIANO WHERE THEY HAD OFTEN GATHERED, HE PLAYED PART OF A FAMILIAR HYMN. ONE PHRASE CALLS GOD, "OUR HOPE FOR YEARS TO COME!" WITH THAT ENCOURAGEMENT, THEY FLED.[1]

That, my friend, is why the Scriptures call hope "an anchor of the soul" (Heb. 6:19). Anchors stabilize; they keep us from drifting. Without an anchor, a boat is at the mercy of the winds and currents. And without an anchor for our souls, we're at the mercy of life's unpredictable weather.

One of the Old Testament words for hope is *tiqvah*, which literally means "a cord" (as an attachment).[2] Even more inter-estingly, this word comes from *qavah,* which means "to bind together by twisting"[3] (such as a braid of hair or a rope). Hope connects. Indeed, it even braids us together with God. It anchors us to the throne of God—"within the veil"—where we are tethered to our faithful High Priest, as an umbilical cord connects a baby in the womb to its mother.

This same Hebrew word is translated "wait" in Isaiah 40:31, "Yet those who wait for the LORD will gain new strength; they will mount up with wings like eagles, they will run and not get tired, they will walk and not become weary." Hoping in God—being anchored and braided to Him—brings renewed strength to run life's race without wearying and to soar above the adversity of life.

Though fleeing for their lives, the Lemkes were running life's race *with* God and therefore with healthy hearts. Unfortunately, unlike the Lemkes, many run *without* hope in God. Consequently, they do so with weak hearts that cannot possibly sustain them in life's race. Hope deferred can weaken our hearts in several ways, causing us to run improperly and, therefore, ineffectively. As part of defining hope deferred and its fruit, let's expose several types of improper running and thereby disarm our enemy in those areas.

After 10 years of waiting for Isaac, Abraham and Sarah succumbed to the relentless barrage of hopelessness. I understand; and I'm sure you do too. Ten years is a long time to wait for a promise, especially when the promise is that you will have a child and you are already old.

As many of us tend to do when hopelessness finally gains the upper hand, Abraham and Sarah took action by *running ahead of God*. These spiritual parents of ours began to speculate how they could fulfill the promise themselves—

without God, if necessary, and maybe even in spite of Him. The result? Ishmael—a son through Hagar, Sarah's Egyptian maid—and a divided family, not to mention centuries of conflict. Running ahead of God creates major problems.

Next Abraham and Sarah did what is also typical: they asked God to accept their connived solution and make it His. "Oh that Ishmael might live before Thee!" Abraham cried out (Gen. 17:18).

HE GIVES US DESTINIES THAT RISE ABOVE ANYTHING WE COULD POSSIBLY PRODUCE ON OUR OWN.

How pathetically human! "I was tired of waiting for Your plan to unfold, God, so I came up with one of my own. Now, please let mine become Yours." Too often our actions demonstrate just that mentality. How many times have I grown impatient when waiting for God's plan to unfold and come up with one of my own? Too many times to count—and you probably have done the same.

But since God knows that His way is always the best way, and His time is always the right time, He refuses to accept our hope-deferred-inspired Ishmaels. He also wants a supernatural element in our destinies that will keep us dependent on Him, and so He gives us destinies that rise above anything we could possibly produce on our own. This isn't unkind on God's part; it is gracious. Who would want to settle for a natural inheritance when they can have a supernatural one? Of course, it's easy to accept these theologically sound and lofty ideas when you're not the one waiting for an Isaac.

If you have run ahead of God and produced an Ishmael or two—and who hasn't—sooner or later the fleshly provision will clash with the spiritual, and Ishmael will have to go (see Gen. 21:9-14). This can be painful. But don't mourn, for "when we have spoiled His plan for us by our folly or ignorance, He has another waiting for us. Every day is a fresh beginning, and the future is radiant with another chance through Him. His imperial voice will bid the dead hopes of yesterday to rise in newness of life and fill the latter days with glorious achievement."[4] This was true of George Frideric Handel, composer of the great oratorio *Messiah*.

> He was a has-been, a fossil, a relic, an old fogy, but it hadn't always been so. As a young man, George Frideric Handel was the talk of England, the best paid composer on earth, and his fame soared around the world.
>
> But the glory passed, audiences dwindled, and one project after another failed. Handel grew depressed. The stress brought on a case of palsy that crippled some of his fingers. "Handel's great days are over," wrote Frederick the Great, "his inspiration is exhausted."

Yet his troubles also matured him, and his music became more heartfelt. One morning Handel received a collection of various biblical texts from Charles Jennens. The opening words from Isaiah 40 moved Handel: *Comfort ye my people.*

On August 22, 1741, he began composing music for the words. Twenty-three days later, the world had *Messiah,* which opened in London to enormous crowds on March 23, 1743. Handel led from his harpsichord, and King George II, who was present that night, surprised everyone by leaping to his feet during the "Hallelujah Chorus." From that day audiences everywhere have stood in reverence during the stirring words: *Hallelujah! And He shall reign forever and ever.*[5]

Aren't you glad Handel let God get rid of his Ishmaels and bring Isaac into the world?

If Satan can't cause us to run ahead of God, he has other results in mind for the hope deferred in our hearts: *running away from God.* Failed expectations can be so devastating and debilitating! Like a balloon that has lost its air, the rapid deflation of our hearts sends our emotions haphazardly spinning out of control. This happened to the disciples. Not expecting things to turn out as they did—the Cross, the Resurrection, the disappearance of Christ—they began the running process.

As Hebrews 6:18-19 tells us, when disappointment and confusion come, our response should be to run *to* the Lord:

RUN WITH HOPE 41

We may have strong encouragement, *we who have fled for refuge in laying hold of the hope set before us*. This hope we have as an anchor of the soul, a hope both sure and steadfast and one which enters within the veil (emphasis added).

The great hymn "The Solid Rock" so eloquently states what our response to adversity should be: "My hope is built on nothing less than Jesus' blood and righteousness." I especially love the verses that state:

When darkness veils His lovely face,
I rest on His unchanging grace.
In every high and stormy gale
My anchor holds within the veil.

His oath, His covenant, His blood,
Support me in the whelming flood.
When all around my soul gives way,
He then is all my hope and stay.[6]

What the disciples should have done in their place of confusion was lay hold of the hope they had found in Christ. What they did was begin a process of running away from God's plan and back to their old lives and vocations: "I am going fishing," impetuous Peter declared (John 21:3).

The other hope-depleted disciples said, in essence, "We're with you, Peter. Enough of this confusing 'save the world' stuff, and enough of crosses and resurrections, then watching Him leave again. It's all a little too confusing for us as well. Now fishing—that we understand! Let's go."

Please understand that they were not just fishing to take a break. They were running from what they couldn't understand and returning to their former occupation. Surely you've been there. Hopelessness and despair disorient us. We lose our bearings, our focus. And sometimes, like the disciples, when we run from the confusion, we don't realize we're running from our purpose and destiny.

I love Christ's response to their confusion. The Scriptures say "that night they caught nothing" (John 21:3). It's a real bummer to stay up all night for nothing. Do you think that was simply bad luck? No way! In His mercy and commitment to them, Christ was saying, "I will not allow you to prosper in running away from Me, back to the old way of life. I'm far too committed to your destiny and My mission to allow that."

Then Christ worked one of His now familiar miracles, telling them to put their net out on the other side of the boat, which resulted in a great catch. What do you suppose He was communicating through these events? Perhaps He wanted them to grasp the following concepts:

- I'm Lord of the fish—*and* the fishermen.
- Even when you don't understand, I want you to trust Me.
- Even though you no longer see Me all the time, I'm still around. Do not fear.

- I told you I would make you fishers of *men,* and I'm guarding that destiny jealously. Now, Peter, rekindle your hope and get back to the race I have for you. Tend My lambs (see John 21:15-17).
- Hope deferred isn't terminal, guys. Hang in there—you'll understand shortly. For now, trust Me.

And so must you and I trust Him. When the plans seem to have changed and He didn't inform you, trust Him. Don't run away. When nothing seems to make sense, He's somewhere near, preparing you a meal that will sustain you until your breakthrough (see John 21:9). Trust Him.

One of my favorite stories in the Bible is of David and Goliath. I love the part when David, after boldly declaring that God would give Goliath into his hands, "ran quickly toward the battle line to meet the Philistine" (1 Sam. 17:48). That's good running! Perhaps this is what David was speaking of in Psalm 18 when he said, "I pursued my enemies and overtook them, and I did not turn back until they were consumed" (v. 37). Our heritage as believers in the Lord is to be bold as a lion, to be on the offensive. The Scriptures teach that our enemies should flee from us, not the other way around (see Deut. 28:7; Prov. 28:1). This fact makes the third result of hope deferred even more tragic: *running from our enemies.*

I'm referring to running from spiritual and emotional giants, of course, not other human beings. There will obviously be times in our lives when we should avoid physical confrontations, if at all possible. Or perhaps, like the Lemkes in our opening story, we may even have to flee from oppressive situations. These we may flee from; spiritual and emotional enemies we should not.

Hope deferred, however, produces fear and makes us uncertain of ourselves, our faith and, yes, even our God. We should be able to move forward in confidence and believe that we are more than conquerors. Instead, at times we find ourselves beginning to operate in fear and timidity, fleeing from the obstacles, the adversities and the giants in our lives.

Hebrews 12:12 tells us to "strengthen . . . the knees that are feeble." "Feeble" is translated from the Greek word *paraluo* from which we get the English word "paralyzed." It's true, isn't it? Fear paralyzes. You've probably heard the phrase "frozen with fear" or the word "petrified," both of which connote that fear immobilizes us. Other translations of this verse bring out the connection between the word *paraluo* and fear: strengthen "your shaky knees"; "stand firm on your shaky legs"; "stiffen the stand of your knocking knees."[7]

Israel's behavior, of course, is the classic example of the paralysis of hopelessness. After experiencing a glorious deliverance from Egypt, wherein God totally emaciated their enemies and showed Himself strong at every point, the Israelites found themselves totally intimidated when they faced the giants of Canaan. They had hoped to see God deal with the Canaanites in the same way He had dealt with the Egyptians, without their having to fight at all. When that did not occur, hope deferred began its paralyzing work, and there was a great erosion of confidence in the hearts of the Israelites.

The next step was predictable, and Israel did what many of us do. As confidence erodes, very often we begin to magnify our enemies' power above our strengths and abilities and, though we wouldn't want to admit it, above that of God's. Hope deferred distorts our vision. Looking at our enemies through hope deferred is like looking at them through a magnifying glass. "We became like grasshoppers in our own sight," the Israeli spies said (Num. 13:33).

Overreaction is usually next. Mark Twain once said, "I am an old man and have known a great many troubles, but most of them have never happened."[8] How true! When fear sets in, we don't act in confidence; rather, we begin to overreact to the situation in which we find ourselves, as did the Israelites:

> Then all the congregation lifted up their voices and cried, and the people wept that night. And all the sons of Israel grumbled against Moses and Aaron; and the whole congregation said to them, "Would that we had died in the land of Egypt! Or would that we had died in this wilderness! And why is the LORD bringing us into this land, to fall by the sword? Our wives and our little ones will become plunder; would it not be better for us to return to Egypt?" So they said to one another, "Let us appoint a leader and return to Egypt" (Num. 14:1-4).

I'm sure you've been there. I know I have. There have been occasions when I'm appalled at how quickly I can go from the mountaintop of victory and great faith to a valley of deep despair and then wonder how I could ever overcome my situation. When this happens, rather than hearing instruction from the Lord and boldly taking action, I find myself cowering in the face of adversity. If this process is not stopped, the giants grow larger while my faith becomes smaller. Slavery in Egypt looks easier than conquering my giants.

We must always remember that the giant we are now facing will always appear to be the biggest. What should we do instead of cowering from these hope-killing Goliaths? Refuse to become hopeless victims. President John F. Kennedy had it right in his showdown with Russia in 1962: "Khrushchev reminds me of the tiger hunter who has picked a place on the wall to hang the tiger skin long before he has caught the tiger. This tiger has other ideas."[9] Thomas Edison also refused to become a victim:

> In December 1914, a great, sweeping fire destroyed Thomas Edison's laboratories in West Orange, New Jersey, wiping out two million dollars' worth of equipment and the record of much of his life's work.
>
> Edison's son Charles ran about frantically trying to find his father. Finally he came upon him, standing near the fire, his face ruddy in the glow, his white hair blown by the winter winds. "My heart ached for him," Charles Edison said. "He was no

longer young, and everything was being destroyed. He spotted me. 'Where's your mother?' he shouted. 'Find her. Bring her here. She'll never see anything like this again as long as she lives.'"

The next morning, walking about the charred embers of so many of his hopes and dreams, the 67-year-old Edison said, *"There is great value in disaster. All our mistakes are burned up. Thank God we can start anew."*[10]

You can't beat a man or a woman who has a hope that strong. To them, God will always be bigger than their giants. Jeremiah, looking at the smoldering ruins of Jerusalem, said much the same thing in Lamentations. Though he lamented, as the name of the book suggests, he did so with hope:

This I recall to my mind, therefore I have hope. Through the Lord's mercies we are not consumed, because His compassions fail not. They are new every morning; great is Your faithfulness. "The LORD is my portion," says my soul, "therefore I hope in Him!" (3:21-24, *NKJV*).

Responses such as these seem contrary to human sanity, and indeed they are. But they reveal the paradoxical nature of an irrepressible trust in God—a hoping against hope, a joy unspeakable and a peace that passes understanding (see Rom. 4:18; Phil. 4:7; 1 Pet. 1:8).

Another form of heart disease that hope deferred creates in us is *running religiously without power*. The Bible speaks of having a form of godliness but denying the power thereof (see 2 Tim. 3:5). The Pharisees were religious—they went through the motions, having the form but losing the reality of the experience. Jesus spoke these words to them, "You are mistaken, not understanding the Scriptures, or the power of God" (Matt. 22:29). Religiosity is knowing the right words—even Scriptures—to say, knowing how to look, walking out Christianity as far as the outward expression is concerned and yet experiencing very little, if any, genuine life—joy, peace, faith or fire—within.

Jesus said of the Church at Sardis in Revelation 3:1-2: "You have a name that you are alive, but you are dead. Wake up, and strengthen the things that remain, which were about to die; for I have not found your deeds completed in the sight of My God." I find it interesting that this church's reputation was still intact. They had a name that they were alive. In other words, among the rest of the Body of Christ, their reputation was still that they were a church alive, perhaps even on fire. We can often fool others with our religiosity, but we can't fool God. Jesus was able to look into their hearts and discern that though they were doing all the right things, having the right form and going through the proper routine of Christianity, inside they were dying. What an incredibly sobering thought!

Zacharias, John the Baptist's father, was a religious hope-deferred victim. He was a priest unto the Lord and was

"righteous . . . walking blamelessly in all the command-
ments and requirements of the Lord" (Luke 1:6). However,
when an angel appeared to him while he was in the Temple
performing the incense offering and told him he and
Elizabeth would have a son, he couldn't believe it. Why?
Hope deferred had set in. He could still perform his religious obligation, but Elizabeth was barren and now they
were old. He could not respond in faith to an angelic visitation and a hope-filled promise that contradicted his hope-
deferred experience up until then.

How often we are like Zacharias! Maybe we haven't run
away from God, and perhaps we're in the "Temple" or
church service every week "performing" like Christians. We
may even be worshiping faithfully, presenting our form of
an incense offering to Him. But if we're honest, many of us
have areas in which hope deferred has eliminated our ability to believe for breakthrough. In that area of our walk with
God, we're merely being religious—having the form yet denying the power.

What an appropriate warning for all of us! There probably is not a Christian alive who hasn't experienced this in
some form. Like the lame man at the pool of Bethesda, we're
still there every day, but we really have no hope within (see
John 5:7). When hope deferred poisons the heart, we still ask
but there's really no faith that we'll receive. We lay hands on
the sick but don't really expect them to recover. We pray for
revival but question if it will actually come. We lift our
hands in worship on Sunday morning, but our hearts are

cold and we think little about the things of God the rest of the week.

Plainly stated, hope deferred, if it doesn't cause us to run away from God, has the potential to make us nothing more than religious in our dealings and relationship with Him. It is Christianity dressed in religious clothing—faithless, perhaps even lifeless, yet looking like the real thing.

If you find yourself in this condition, don't yield to condemnation, and don't give up. This is a book about overcoming hope deferred, not yielding to it. There is always a way to victory in God. Before you finish this book, your heart can be well. Persevere! You are an overcomer in the deepest part of your spiritual DNA, "for everyone born of God overcomes the world. This is the victory that has overcome the world, even our faith" (1 John 5:4, *NIV*).

The last of the five results of hope deferred, which I don't want to say much about, is an extreme one. You are not there or you wouldn't be reading this book. This extreme result, however, should at least be mentioned as a warning. Judas, who had a terminal case of hope deferred, is the best example of *running with God's enemies*. This behavior results in denying God and turning away from Him altogether.

Believing that the Messiah would overthrow the Roman government and set up an earthly throne of His own (and by the way, all of the disciples thought the same thing), Judas became incredibly disillusioned when he saw that Jesus was not going to do this. Hope deferred then set in, poisoning his heart, and he found himself a betrayer, cavorting with the enemies of Christ.

Certainly this is an extreme result of hope deferred, but it is a potential that all of us must realize exists. If we allow hope deferred to create bitterness toward the Lord, then we run the risk of completely turning away from Him.

If you find yourself suffering from any level of hope deferred, and a sick heart, don't give up and don't be intimidated. In the book *The Ten Laws of Lasting Love*, Paul Pearsall relates an occasion in his fight against cancer when he and his wife had to overcome a vicious attack of hope deferred.

Any time a doctor came with news of my progress, my wife would join with me in a mutual embrace. The reports were seldom good during the early phases of my illness, and one day a doctor brought particularly frightening news. Gazing at his clipboard, he murmured, "It doesn't look like you're going to make it."

Before I could ask a question of this doomsayer, my wife stood up, handed me my robe, adjusted the tubes attached to my body and said, "Let's get out of here. This man is a risk to your health." As she helped me struggle to the door, the doctor approached us. "Stay back," demanded my wife. "Stay away from us."

As we walked together down the hall, the doctor attempted to catch up with us. "Keep going," said my wife, pushing the intravenous stand. "We're going to talk to someone who really knows what is going on." Then she held up her hand to the doctor. "Don't come any closer to us."

The two of us moved as one. We fled to the safety and hope of a doctor who did not confuse diagnosis with verdict.[11]

Don't confuse diagnosis with verdict! Refuse to listen to hopelessness. You may be suffering the effects of hope deferred, but you will recover. Have the attitude of the small bird in the midst of a storm that "was clinging to the limb of a tree, seemingly calm and unafraid. As the wind tore at the limbs of the tree, the bird continued to look the storm in the face, as if to say, 'Shake me off; I still have wings.'"[12]

You do have wings; you can, and will, fly!

CHAPTER 3

THERE IS
MUSIC IN YOU
STILL

It was a chilly fall day when the farmer spied the little sparrow lying on its back in the middle of his field. The farmer stopped his plowing, looked down at the frail, feathered creature and inquired, "Why are you lying upside down like that?"

"I heard the sky is going to fall today," replied the bird.

The old farmer chuckled. "And I suppose your spindly little legs can hold up the sky?"

"One does what one can," replied the plucky sparrow.[1]

I'm always amazed at how God uses spindly little humans to get things accomplished. The apostle Paul understood this. He said that God's "strength is made perfect in weakness" (2 Cor. 12:9, *KJV*). Gideon understood it, too. He and 300 soldiers faced an army of 135,000, using torches and pitchers as weapons (see Judg. 6—8). I'd call that a spindly little army. It reminds me of the phrase used in Romans 4:18 to describe Abraham: "In hope against hope he believed."

If I understand that phrase correctly, it means that when there was absolutely no hope, Abraham hoped anyway. Zodhiates says it means "in spite of" or "without ground of hope."[2] With no grounds for hope, in spite of the impossibility of the situation, Abraham hoped anyway. It's sort of like the "but God" phrases in Scripture. There are many; here are a couple:

> And as for you, you meant evil against me [Joseph], *but God* meant it for good in order to bring about this present result, to preserve many people alive (Gen. 50:20, emphasis added).

> "And now shall I [Samson] die of thirst and fall into the hands of the uncircumcised?" *But God* split the hollow place that is in Lehi so that water came out of it. When he drank, his strength returned and he revived (Judg. 15:18-19, emphasis added).

The point is that at times no human hope or ability exists in a particular situation, *but God* shows up! That's what He wants to do in your life—enter your hopeless scenario and invade your hope-deferred world. In this chapter we begin to facilitate that process. So, like Abraham, go ahead and dare to hope against hope. After all, isn't that what faith is—believing in something you can't see or that doesn't seem to exist?

The story is told of a discouraged man in London who was on his way to drown himself. At that moment life did not seem worth living. On his way along the street he stopped and looked at a picture in a shop window. It was Watts's "Hope." It is a picture of a woman, blindfolded, sitting on top of the world. Her lyre has but one string; yet still hoping and believing the instrument will make music, she is ready to strike it.

The bewildered man, as he stood looking, said to himself: "Well, I have one string—I have a little boy at home." So he turned and went back to his boy.

When we feel that life has little left, let us take stock. We will always find we have something left. We always have God left. That was the way Habakkuk felt. The flock might be cut off from the stall; there might be no fruit in the orchard; the hillsides might be bare; but he had God left. There was music possible yet (see Hab. 3:17-19).[3]

And there is music left in you! I know you can play hope's song, even in the dark night of the soul. Job, in his hellish suffering, said the Lord "gives songs in the night" (Job 35:10). David, during his time of exile, said, "His song will be with me in the night" (Ps. 42:8). Paul and Silas, beaten, bleeding and in chains, "about midnight . . . were praying and singing hymns of praise to God" (Acts 16:25). There is hope in the night; and there is music somewhere in your soul. Don't give up.

Back to Gideon and his spindly little army. There is a hope-deferred healing coming in this story! Israel, because of their sin, was being oppressed by the Midianites. Sometimes we're responsible for the hope deferred in our lives; sometimes we're victims. This situation had clearly been created by the Israelites themselves. But God is a God of great mercy, and He was about to bring deliverance.

As He often does, God chose as His instrument a person who appeared to be very unqualified for the task. Gideon certainly wasn't a man of great faith or hope at this point in his life. In fact, when the Lord called him a valiant warrior (see Judg. 6:12), Gideon's hope deferred became very obvious. His response was filled with unbelief and even cynicism:

> Then Gideon said to him, "O my lord, *if* the LORD is with us, *why* then has all this happened to us? And *where* are all His miracles which our fathers told us about, saying, 'Did not the LORD bring us up from Egypt?' But now *the LORD has abandoned us* and given us into the hand of Midian" (Judg. 6:13, emphasis added).

Gideon's, and all of Israel's, heartsick, hope-deferred condition had progressed to the point where, for the most part, they had finally abandoned worship of Jehovah and were now serving the false gods of Baal and Asherah. Isn't that so typical of many of us? We may not set up literal idols, as Israel did, but we often waver in our devotion to God and begin to place our trust in other things instead: ourselves, other people, money, government, drugs, alcohol, pleasures, success and maybe even other religions.

Notice, however, the precious response of the Lord to this condition that plagued Gideon and the Israelites. God was about to reveal Himself to them in a new way—as the God who heals hope deferred. Gideon decided to offer a sacrifice to his angelic visitor. While he was doing so, fire sprang up from the rock upon which he had laid the sacrifice and consumed his offering. Gideon, of course, was terrified by this awesome display of power. But the angel said to him, "Peace [*Shalom*] to you" (Judg. 6:23).

Most of us have a very limited understanding of this word translated as "peace." While it does indeed mean peace in the sense that we normally think, it includes far more than that. The basic concept contained in this word is completeness or wholeness. As Zodhiates says, "it is a sense of well being; . . . to be unharmed or unhurt; . . . it expresses completeness, harmony and fulfillment."[4]

What the angel of the Lord literally said to Gideon was, "Wholeness to you, Gideon." While the angel was no doubt attempting to alleviate Gideon's temporary and immediate fear of him, I believe he was also bringing healing and release to him in a general sense. Gideon was so moved by this experience that he built an altar to the Lord and called it Jehovah Shalom, which became one of the popular redemption names of the Lord. It means "the Lord our wholeness." I don't think this would have been done to commemorate a comforting word meant only for one brief moment.

Hope deferred was lifted off of Gideon. God's holy and awesome presence was healing him. God wants to do that for you as well. He wants to visit you in your hope-deferred state. He wants to invade your insecure world of pain, despair and disillusionment, bringing fire from His altar, and speak a word of wholeness to you. It may come through a sermon, a friend, Scripture or the quiet voice of the Lord in your heart; but of this you can be certain: God has a healing word for you. For Sherry, in the following story, it came in a most unusual way.

Sherry was visiting another city when she noticed a gloriously beautiful sunset. Wanting to share it with someone, she asked a clerk in a nearby store to come outside. Obviously puzzled, the woman followed her outside.

"Just look at that sunset!" Sherry said. "God's in His heaven and all's right with the world." After briefly enjoying the beauty, the clerk went back inside and Sherry left.

Four years later, Sherry was recently divorced, on her own for the first time, living in reduced circumstances, and feeling very discouraged. She read a magazine article about a woman who had been in similar circumstances. This woman had come to the end of a marriage, moved to a strange community, worked at a job she didn't like, and was struggling. Then something happened. A woman came into her store and asked her to step outside. The stranger pointed to the sunset and said, "God's in His heaven and all's right with the world." Realizing the truth in that statement, she turned her life around.

Sherry's perspective changed, too—the gift of hope came full circle.[5]

GOD KNOWS WHAT EACH OF US NEEDS TO HEAR AND WHEN WE NEED TO HEAR IT. KEEP LISTENING.

Sherry's healing word did indeed come in a most unusual way and through an even more surprising vessel—herself. God knows what each of us needs to hear and when we need to hear it. Keep listening. Just as He spoke to Sherry and to Gideon, He will speak to you.

At this point in Gideon's story, when the offer of wholeness came, he had a choice. So will we. Gideon could have stopped the process right there, saying, "I'm not ready for this." He could have allowed his past frustrations, pains, fears and diseased heart to keep him from progressing toward hope. He faced a crisis point we all reach in the process of healing from hope deferred: choose life or choose death.

Hope is a choice that must be made. Experiencing hope deferred does not require a choice—pain and disappointment are facts of life—but *healing* does. *Choosing to hope again is the first step toward healing.*

Wilma Rudolph, three-time gold medalist in the 1960 Olympics and once known in the field of running as the world's fastest woman, said, "The doctors told me I would never walk again, but my mother told me I would, so I believed my mother."[6] Born prematurely into a very poor family, and the twentieth of 22 children, Wilma was not permitted to receive care at the local white hospital. For the next several years, her mother nursed her through many illnesses. When Wilma contracted polio, her mother took her twice a week for two years to the nearest medical facility that would treat her—it was 50 miles away from home. Wilma Rudolph's life is a story of achievement against the odds; but the story began with the right choices.[7]

Like this Olympic champion, we must choose to hope. I realize this puts responsibility on us, but it also brings us an incredibly liberating truth. Healing—getting free from hope deferred—is a choice that can be made. The Scriptures are filled with statements that let us know we have the power of choice and can choose life over death. The Lord told the Israelites to "choose life" (see Deut. 30:19). We choose how we will respond to devastating circumstances, as seen in the following story.

William Carey, the "Father of Modern Missions," wanted to translate the Bible into as many Indian languages as possible. Early in 1832, his associate discovered flames engulfing their printing room. Although workers fought the blaze, everything was destroyed.

The next day, another missionary traveled to Carey's location. "I can think of no easy way to break the news," he said. "The printshop burned to the ground last night."

Carey was stunned. His complete library was gone, including dictionaries, grammar books and Bibles, as well as typesets for fourteen languages.

"The work of years—gone in a moment," he whispered.

He took little time to mourn. "The loss is heavy," he wrote, "but . . . we are not discouraged, indeed the work is already begun again in every language. We are *cast down but not in despair*."

News of the fire catapulted Carey to instant fame in England. Funds were raised and volunteers offered to help. By the end of 1832, portions of Scripture, even entire Bibles, had been issued in forty-four languages and dialects.

The secret of Carey's success was his resiliency. "There are grave difficulties on every hand," he once wrote, "and more are looming ahead. Therefore we must go forward."[8]

William Carey made the right choice. He stared adversity

and lack in the face and said, "There is a song in this night." You can do the same. Don't wait another moment. Do it *now*! You don't have to be well to hope, but you do have to hope to become well.

At this point in Gideon's process (see Judg. 6:25-27), he was required to do something else to seal his healing and become qualified to deliver the rest of his people. Israel had become idolatrous, and the village altar to Baal and Asherah was in Gideon's very own backyard. Baal was a god of fertility, rain (and therefore vegetation), sun and war.[9] Asherah was a goddess associated with passion and the sea. According to some, she was the wife of El and the mother of Baal.[10]

Israel had transferred their trust from Jehovah to these gods, worshiping them in order to

EVERY FEAR, EVERY WALL YOU'VE PUT UP TO PROTECT YOUR HEART, EVERY PLACE WHERE YOU'VE DECIDED THAT YOU WON'T TRUST GOD, TEAR IT DOWN.

receive the benefits they were believed to provide. In essence, the Israelites were saying, "Since You haven't come through for us, Jehovah, we're going to put our trust in Baal and Asherah."

God told Gideon to tear down the altars built for these false gods. He was showing Gideon that to be truly whole and for Israel to be delivered, their faith and trust had to be transferred back to Him. Gideon obeyed, though he did so in the middle of the night because he feared the rest of the village. Hope and faith do not have to be operating fully to move us in the right direction. We must begin with what we have. And like Gideon, *a part of our healing process is to tear down and annihilate everything other than God in which we have placed our trust.* Anything we bow before, allowing it control in our lives, could be classified as an idol. Many people have bowed to fear, unbelief, insecurity, past wounds, rejection, hopelessness, bitterness and a host of other things.

Every fear, every wall you've put up to protect your heart, every place where you've decided (even if it was unconsciously) that you won't trust God, tear it down. Every subtle determination not to believe, every testimonial to disappointment that exists in your heart, right now, by faith, tear it down. You must do this to make way for God to become Jehovah Shalom to you.

The next event in Gideon's story is so beautiful it's almost too good to be true. The Lord instructed Gideon to use the wood from the altars to Baal and Asherah to build the fire on which to offer Him a sacrifice. He didn't say to burn the idolatrous altars and *then* offer Him a sacrifice. *Please, don't miss this.* He was demonstrating to Gideon—and to us as well—"I won't waste your sin, pain, disillusionment or hopelessness. I intend to destroy them all; but in the process, I plan to use them as a part of your transformation.

Offer them to Me as kindling and allow your deliverance from them to light a new fire of worship to Me."

Imagine it, God using even our idols! Too good to be true? No. God wants to use even our mistakes and failures, transforming them into altars of worship. He overcomes evil with good and makes even the wrath of man praise Him (see Rom. 12:21; Ps. 76:10).

Resist condemnation and shame. "There is therefore now no condemnation for those who are in Christ Jesus" (Rom. 8:1). There comes a time when we must believe that God is not only bigger than our hurts but that He is also bigger than our mistakes and unbelief—even those things we have brought on ourselves. The Scriptures are filled with examples of people who have made very serious errors, and yet God was able to redeem and heal them. We must realize that God is merciful and able to deliver us even from the pain we bring upon ourselves. He came to love and to heal sinners, not just the righteous.

Jesus accepted the title "Son of David," even though it made Him the son of an adulterer and a murderer. Abraham made some very grave mistakes, and yet the end result of his life was that he was called the friend of God. The disciples abandoned Jesus at His greatest hour of need, and yet a few days later they became the leaders of His new movement called the Church. Peter denied the Lord with a curse; but just a few days later he was used to heal a lame man and preach a sermon that led 3,000 people to be born again. God can and does redeem us from our past.

We sometimes refer to our difficult times, such as the one Gideon and Israel experienced, as winter seasons. The river of God's Holy Spirit in Ezekiel 47, which produces life and healing everywhere it goes, is also associated with a winter season. The word for "river" in the passage is *nachal*, which means "a stream, especially a winter torrent."[11] Some streams and rivers are dry during certain times of the year; but they fill up when there is rain or, as in this case, when the spring thaw melts the snow and ice on the mountains. Tiny rivulets develop that come together to form streams and eventually become *nachalim* (rivers). Though Ezekiel's "winter river" began as a trickle in verse 1, it eventually became a mighty unfordable river by verse 5.

The changing seasons are a powerful and comforting picture of the God who uses the snow and ice of our spiritual winters to bring deep flows of His Spirit to us in the next season. The season is changing

- for those who are confused and disillusioned;
- for the heart grieving from the pain of loss;
- for the faithful but weary soldier whose streambed is dry;
- for those who have lost their first love;
- for the Gideons of this world who are heartsick with hope deferred.

Yes, the season is changing—it is time for the spring thaw!

Winter doesn't last forever. God is ready to bring the fire of His presence to consume the sacrifice and melt the ice and snow of your winter. The river will flow *to* you and eventually *through* you. Hope deferred will end. Despair will yield to His command: "Wholeness to you!" Oppression will lift and joy will return.

A passage in the Song of Solomon is for all hope-deferred victims:

> My beloved responded and said to me, "Arise, my darling, my beautiful one, and come along. For behold, the winter is past, the rain is over and gone. The flowers have already appeared in the land; the time has arrived for pruning the vines, and the voice of the turtledove has been heard in our land. The fig tree has ripened its figs, and the vines in blossom have given forth their fragrance. Arise, my darling, my beautiful one, and come along!" (2:10-13).

Psalm 51 was written by a hope-deferred sinner named David who had recently committed adultery and murder: "God, make a fresh start in me, shape a Genesis week from the chaos of my life. Bring me back from gray exile, put a fresh wind in my sails!" (vv. 10, 12, *THE MESSAGE*).

God is ready to do just that for each of us.

Become not a Baal worshiper but a Baal conqueror. Gideon's name was changed to Jerubbaal, meaning "Baal conqueror," after he tore down the altar of Baal (see Judg. 7:1). That is your destiny as well—to conquer every idol, overcome every fear and be healed of hope deferred.

A glorious verse in Romans summarizes this beautiful truth that God wants to take the pain, the hurts, the evil in our lives and bring good from them. It's one of the most famous verses in the entire Bible: "And we know that God causes all things to work together for good to those who love God, to those who are called according to His purpose" (8:28).

This rich verse, filled with hope, contains two Greek words I want to emphasize. The phrase "work together" is the Greek word *sunergeo*, from which we get the wonderful words "synergy" and "synergism." Synergism is "the combined action of two or more which have a greater total effect than the sum of their individual effects."[12] God is promising that He will take all of the bad, all of the evil, every attempt of the enemy to destroy your faith—indeed to destroy your life—and through His miraculous power use those things to make something good. In other words, pain *plus* devastation *plus* despair *plus* difficulty *plus* loss *equal* good! Incredible! *But God!* That truth alone has the power to heal you of hope deferred.

When complimented on her homemade biscuits, the cook at a popular Christian conference center told Dr. Harry Ironside, "Just consider what goes into the making of these biscuits. The flour itself doesn't taste good, neither does the baking powder, nor the shortening, nor the other ingredients. However, when I mix them all together and put them in the oven, they come out just right."

Much of life seems tasteless, even bad, but God
is able to combine these ingredients of our life in
such a way that "good" results.[13]

And He does not simply turn them into just any "good,"
by the way, but *agathos* good! If the Greek word *kalos* had
been used, it would have meant "constitutionally good,"
something well made that perhaps looks good but may not
have any practical purpose. But the word that is used in
Romans 8:28, *agathos,* means "good and profitable; useful;
beneficial."[14]

The Lord is not referring to a synergistic work that we can
"put a good face on" or perhaps even say, "It's okay," giving an
outward expression or an appearance that everything is all
right when inwardly we're still disabled. No way. He promises
to so transform all of the bad in our lives that it is changed
into good fruit, good works, usefulness or profitability.

It's somewhat like a pregnancy. Very few, if any, of the
changes that occur to a woman's body during pregnancy
could be described as good. But, oh, the beauty of what is
growing inside and will one day be seen! This illustration
captures the point:

A mother, the instant that she knows she is with
child, lives her every moment in anticipation of
delivery. After a time she cannot take a step, make a
move, think a thought that is disassociated from
the coming of her child.

In America, people are supposed to ignore the obvious fact that a woman is with child. In France the case is quite the contrary. If a man is introduced to a woman who is an expectant mother, it is the height of politeness for him to congratulate her. *"Je vous félicite de votre esperance"*—"I congratulate you on your hope"—is a common phrase among the cultured.[15]

I know that hope deferred is being broken off of you. Your heart is being healed and you are becoming pregnant with hope. Congratulations!

CHAPTER 4

TELL YOUR
HEART TO BEAT
AGAIN

In his book *Lee: The Last Years*, Charles Bracelen Flood reports that after the Civil War, Robert E. Lee visited a Kentucky lady who took him to the remains of a grand old tree in front of her house. There she bitterly cried that its limbs and trunk had been destroyed by federal artillery fire. She looked to Lee for a word condemning the North or at least sympathizing with her loss.

After a brief silence, Lee said, "Cut it down, my dear Madam, and forget it."[1]

We are in the process of cutting down our trees scarred from the enemy's artillery fire of hope deferred. There is "a time to weep, and a time to laugh; a time to mourn, and a time to dance" (Eccles. 3:4). It's time to dance! Rubem Alves once said, "Hope is hearing the melody of the future. Faith is to dance to it."[2]

The following fascinating narrative about dancing is appropriate for hope-deferred sufferers:

Imagine you and the Lord Jesus are walking down the road together. For much of the way, the Lord's footprints go along steadily, consistently, rarely varying the pace. But your footprints are a disorganized stream of zigzags, starts, stops, turnarounds, circles, departures, and returns. For much of the way, it seems to go like this, but gradually your footprints come more in line with the Lord's, soon paralleling His consistently. You and Jesus are walking as true friends!

This seems perfect, but then an interesting thing happens. Your footprints, that once etched the sand next to Jesus', are now walking precisely in His steps. Inside His larger footprints are your smaller ones; safely you and Jesus are becoming one.

This goes on for many miles, but gradually you notice another change. The footprints inside the large footprints seem to grow larger. Eventually they disappear altogether. There is only one set of footprints; they have become one. This goes on for a long time, but suddenly the second set of footprints is back.

This time it seems even worse! Zigzags all over the place. Stops. Starts. Gashes in the sand. A veritable mess of prints. You are amazed and shocked. Your dream ends.

Now you pray: "Lord, I understand the first scene with zigzags and fits. I was a new Christian; I was just learning. But You walked on through the storm and helped me learn to walk with you."

And He spoke softly, "That is correct."

"And when the smaller footprints were inside of Yours, I was actually learning to walk in Your steps; followed You very closely."

And He answered, "Very good. You have understood everything so far."

"When the smaller footprints grew and filled in Yours, I suppose that I was becoming like You in every way."

And He beamed. "Precisely."

"So, Lord, was there a regression or something? The footprints separated, and this time it was worse than at first."

There is a pause as the Lord answers with a smile in His voice, "You didn't know? That was when we danced!"[3]

Hebrews 10:19-23 gives us music to dance to in this healing process as we recover from hope deferred:

Since therefore, brethren, we have confidence to enter the holy place by the blood of Jesus, by a new and living way which He inaugurated for us through the veil, that is, His flesh, and since we have a great priest over the house of God, let us draw near with a sincere heart in full assurance of faith, having our hearts sprinkled clean from an evil conscience and our bodies washed with pure water. *Let us hold fast the confession of our hope without wavering,* for He who promised is faithful (emphasis added).

Several important steps to having a healthy heart are found in this passage on hoping in God's faithfulness, the first of which is to "draw near" to the Lord. The book of James also tells us to "draw near to God and He will draw near to you" (Jas. 4:8). This is perhaps the most important point in our healing process. You must find your hope within the veil (see Heb. 6:18-19). When we position ourselves next to the Lord, the circumstances around us lose significance in comparison to His presence. The storms of life are no longer our point of reference when He is our focal point, as illustrated in the following story:

> THE STORMS OF LIFE ARE NO LONGER OUR POINT OF REFERENCE WHEN HE IS OUR FOCAL POINT.

In Robert Louis Stevenson's story of a storm, he describes a ship caught off a rocky coast, threatening death to all on board. One of the terrified passengers made his way to the pilothouse, where the pilot was lashed to his post with his hands on the wheel, turning the ship little by little into the open sea. The pilot smiled at the man, who then rushed back to the deck below, shouting, "I have seen the face of the pilot and he smiled. All is well." The sight of that smiling face averted panic and converted despair into hope.[4]

We must draw near to the Lord in order to see Him there at the point of our pain. It is in His presence that healing comes and we experience fullness of joy (see Ps. 16:11).

One of the ways we draw near is through praise and worship. I know it sounds terribly simplistic—and I would never make light of your pain—but I believe that any person's life could be radically and forever changed by extreme doses of praise and worship. Simply applying worship in the same way that one would therapy—taking an hour or two each day and declaring the greatness of God—would create a place for the Lord to set up His throne in our hearts (see Ps. 22:3). From there He would be able to rule over the areas of hurt.

Look up Scriptures that describe God's healing power, His mercies and love; then praise Him by declaring these Scriptures over yourself. Do this for 15-minute increments throughout the day until an hour or two each day is spent worshiping God. Hope deferred could never survive such an onslaught of power and the presence of God. Psalm 107:20 tells us that God's Word can actually be a medicine.

David, whose sin with Bathsheba cost him the life of their newborn child, drew near to the Lord for forgiveness and healing (see Ps. 51). Praise, humility and repentance overcame not only sin but also hope deferred. David also drew near to God for victory over hope deferred while he was in the cave of Adullam. As mentioned in chapter 1, after having fled from Saul and finding himself an outcast from Israel, David made this, and probably other caves, his home for a few years. Psalm 27, written during this painful season, talks about drawing near to the Lord in his place of pain:

> One thing I have asked from the LORD, that I shall seek: that I may dwell in the house of the LORD all the days of my life, to behold the beauty of the LORD, and to meditate in His temple. For in the day of trouble He will conceal me in His tabernacle; in the secret place of His tent He will hide me; He will lift me up on a rock (vv. 4-5).

Many other psalms were written during this season of David's life. He knew the power of drawing near to God, and that's what most of these psalms are about. Use some of them—or compose your own—to draw near to the Lord. If we move into a life of radically drawing near to Him during our time of pain, especially through praise and worship, we will see change almost immediately.

The next healing step in this passage from Hebrews 10 is found in verse 23, which tells us to "hold fast the confession of our hope without wavering." Psalm 107:2 says, "Let the redeemed of the LORD say so." I know it may seem difficult to understand or, again, very simplistic, but a tremendous key to our healing from hope deferred is simply to begin to say out loud what God says about us. There is great power in speaking the Word of God to our hearts.

During an open-heart surgery that my brother, Tim, was allowed to witness, the patient's heart had been stopped from beating. However, when it came time to restart it, despite repeated attempts, the medical staff was unable to get the heart to beat again. Finally, although the patient was obviously unconscious, the surgeon leaned over and said into the patient's ear, "We need your help. We cannot get your heart going. Tell your heart to start beating." Immediately, as incredible as it sounds, the patient's heart began to beat again.

Yours can beat again too if you'll hold fast to your confession of hope. The word for "confession" in Hebrews 10 is *homologia*, which simply means "saying the same thing as." Biblical confession is nothing more or less than saying what God says about you. You must tell your heart to live by speaking truth—God's Word—to it. And, yes, even by commanding it to beat again.

Declaring what God's Word says about us when our circumstances seem contradictory may appear like a refusal to accept reality. But I believe there is good denial and bad denial. Bad denial is trying to live life by burying our emotions or simply trying to act like we're okay when we're not. An example of this is seen in the following:

The story is told of a great, never-say-die general who was taken captive and thrown into a deep, wide pit along with a number of his soldiers. In that pit was a huge pile of horse manure.

"Follow me," the general cried to his men as he dove into the pile. "There has to be a horse in here somewhere!"[5]

About the only positive thing that can be said about this general is that at least he was enough of a leader to go first. This story illustrates bad denial at its worst; it makes about as much sense as some of the ways in which we think we can bury our emotional pain.

The good denial I am referring to is when in spite of what we feel or what our circumstances say, we choose to believe the truth of God's Word and what He says about us. We allow it to transform our situation and heal us. This isn't denying the *reality* of our circumstances but, rather, denying *their right to remain in control* of our lives.

This may be difficult for you to hear, but it's not what happens to us that controls us or affects us so negatively. Rather, *it is what we believe about the situation* that controls us. That's one of the reasons a person can experience a particular pain, such as betrayal or loss, and recover relatively quickly; and yet, another person will not be able to do so. Holding fast to what God says about us enables us to believe the right thing.

When the obstacles that bring about hope deferred threaten to destroy us, we must align ourselves with God's perspective in order to avert disaster. Steve Fossett

recognized the need to reposition himself instead of allowing his surroundings to control him:

> On January 13, 1997, Steve Fossett climbed into the
> cockpit of a hot-air balloon with the ambition of
> being the first to circle the globe in a balloon. After
> three days he had crossed the Atlantic and was fly-
> ing eastward over Africa.
>
> The prevailing wind carried him on a direct
> course for the country of Libya. But Libya had
> refused permission to fly in its air space, which
> meant he could be shot down. Balloons cannot
> turn; so when a change of direction is needed, they
> must change altitude to find a crosswind blowing
> in a different direction.
>
> Fossett dropped 6,300 feet, where a southeast
> wind blew. He safely skirted Libya, then heated the
> balloon, rose 10,000 feet and caught an easterly
> wind, which carried him back on course.
>
> Bertrand Piccard, another balloonist, sees a sim-
> ilarity between balloon flight and daily life: "In the
> balloon you are prisoners of the wind and go only in
> its direction. In life people think they are prisoners of
> circumstance. But in the balloon, as in life, you can
> change altitude, and when you change altitude, you
> change direction. You are not a prisoner anymore."
>
> A person changes altitude by changing atti-
> tude.[6]

What a wonderful truth! We are not prisoners of the winds of adversity. Holding fast to what God says about us is one of the ways we change altitude and attitude. It is good denial, which in essence says, "In spite of what the winds of adversity have said to me, I'm going to go in another direction—God's." We must find the current of the Holy Spirit, which is what God says about us in His Word, and soar with Him to victory.

The word for "holding fast" is consistent with this thought and actually means "to set one's course." The word is used this way in Acts 27 when the boat Paul was on set its course for a particular direction, in spite of a storm. When we take what God says about us in His Word and begin to agree by saying the same thing, it enables us to overcome the storms of life and stay on God's course for us.

One of Paul's spiritual sons, Timothy, had been blown somewhat off course by difficult times. In 2 Timothy 1:6-7, Paul was helping him get back on course: "And for this reason I remind you to kindle afresh the gift of God which is in you through the laying on of my hands. For God has not given us a spirit of timidity, but of power and love and discipline." This passage has some timely lessons for us concerning our healing process from hope deferred.

Paul exhorted Timothy to kindle afresh the gift that had been put in him, and then encouraged him that God had not given him a spirit of fear. The word "timidity" (*deilia*), translated as "fear" in the *King James Version*, is not the normal word for a phobia, but a word that implies insecurity. Timothy had evidently allowed insecurity to cause the gifts in him to shut down.

Paul went on to tell Timothy that God had given him a spirit of power, love and discipline. Discipline—*sophronismos*—is an incredibly powerful word for us in our healing process from hope deferred. This is a word composed of two root words, *sozo* and *phrao*. *Sozo* is the very important New Testament word for "salvation." It implies total salvation, covering wholeness, healing, safety, preservation and everything else included in our salvation.

The other root word, *phrao*, means "to rein in or curb the feelings or thoughts of the mind." When you put these two words together, which is what Paul did for Timothy, the thought conveyed is that we are not to let anything—negative feelings, emotions or thoughts—cause us to be ruled by fear or insecurity. Instead we are to rein in these thoughts and emotions through the power of the salvation (wholeness) we have received. Paul was saying to Timothy, "Let the salvation of the Lord in you empower you to rein in the negative thoughts and feelings of the mind."

You can see why the word is translated "discipline"; but even this is not a strong enough translation. No one word could be. The discipline of which Paul is speaking is not achieved through human will power alone, but because there is a salvation—a wholeness—deep inside of us that God has placed there. We must allow that salvation to rise up, enabling us to rein in the thoughts of fear, doubt and insecurity that try to control us. Romans 15:13 states that we can "abound in hope *by the power of the Holy Spirit*" (emphasis added).

- When fear encroaches, let the salvation of God within enable you to rein it in.
- When you feel intimidated, let the salvation of God within enable you to rein it in.
- When hopeless thoughts try to crowd out faith, let the salvation of God within enable you to rein it in.
- When the enemy of your soul tells you that you aren't going to make it, let the salvation of God within enable you to rein it in.

Hebrews 10 has yet another key principle that will be a part of our healing process. Verse 24 says, "And let us consider how to stimulate one another to love and good deeds." We must always remember that God and His healing power flow to us, in part, through other people.

In this context of holding fast to our hope, the Lord speaks of the need to give and receive encouragement. "Consider" is the word *katanoeo*, which means "to think about something intensely."[7] *Noeo* involves the concept of thinking or using the mind. The prefix, *kata*, however, intensifies it to where it is not a casual thought, but contemplation or considering. "Give serious thought to how you can help others," the Lord tells us.

And how are we to help one another? We "stimulate" (*paroxusmos*) others to love and good deeds. The word means "incitement to good, or to dispute something in anger."[8] Therefore, it means to provoke or incite, either for good or for bad—to stimulate someone in a good way, or to cause contention. It is composed of *para*, which means "to be beside, with, or near," and *oxus*, which means "sharp." Literally, the word would mean "to sharpen alongside."

In other words, in its positive sense, it means to come alongside someone in order to provoke them in a good way or to sharpen their skills and abilities. It is probably what the Scripture in Proverbs 27:17 refers to when it says, "Iron sharpens iron, so one man sharpens another."

Verse 25 then gives the crowning phrase, "encouraging one another." I know it seems like a simple, insignificant phrase; but it isn't. Encourage—*parakaleo*—means "to call to one's side, hence aid."[9] It comes from the same root words as *Paraclete*, which is one of the names of the Holy Spirit. In the same way the Holy Spirit has been sent to come alongside and help us, we are exhorted to do so for one another. Or we could say the *Paraclete* (Holy Spirit) *parakeleos* through us. We are to give intense thought as to how we can come alongside one another, sharpening and giving aid.

The Bible says we are to bear one another's burdens and to bear with one another (see Gal. 6:2; Eph. 4:2; Col. 3:13). Two words are used for "bearing" in the New Testament, one of which is *anechomai*. This is the word for bearing up or staking ourselves next to another, so they don't fall—much as a person would tie a stake to a tomato plant to sustain it against the weight it carries. The strength of the stake is transferred to the plant and thus "bears it up." When the Lord commands us to bear with one another in Colossians 3:13 and Ephesians 4:2, He isn't simply saying, "Put up with one another."

Although He is telling us to do that, He is also saying, "Stake yourselves to one another." In other words, we're to come alongside a brother or sister who is weighed down and say, "You're not going to fall and be broken or destroyed, because I'm staking myself to you. My strength is now yours. Go ahead, lean on me. As long as I can stand, you will too." What a wonderful picture for the Body of Christ. Fruit will result; hope deferred and heart disease will be cured.

See to it that someone makes it because of you. Hebrews 12:15 says, "See to it that no one comes short of the grace of God; that no root of bitterness springing up causes trouble, and by it many be defiled." "See to it" is *episkopeo*, a word for shepherding, overseeing or doing the work of a bishop. "Shepherd, or bishop, one another," He is saying to us. Care for each other; make sure no one misses God's grace.

Jackie Robinson was the first black to play major league baseball. While breaking baseball's color barrier, he faced jeering crowds in every stadium. One day, while playing in his home stadium in Brooklyn, he committed an error. His own fans began to ridicule him. He stood at second base, humiliated, while the fans jeered. Then shortstop "Pee Wee" Reese came over and stood next to him. He put his arm around Jackie Robinson and faced the crowd. The fans grew quiet. Robinson later said that arm around his shoulder saved his career.[10]

Place your arm around someone; see to it that they make it. Allow the Holy Spirit to minister God's grace through you. And if you are in need of help, be open and humble enough to receive it. God has an arm for you.

CHAPTER 5

HOREB WON'T ALWAYS BE HORRIBLE

CRAIG RANDALL DRIVES A GARBAGE TRUCK IN PEABODY, MASSACHUSETTS. IN A GARBAGE CONTAINER ONE DAY, HE NOTICED A WENDY'S SOFT DRINK CUP BEARING A CONTEST STICKER. HAVING WON A CHICKEN SANDWICH THE WEEK BEFORE, RANDALL CHECKED IT, HOPING FOR SOME FRENCH FRIES OR A SOFT DRINK.

INSTEAD, HE PEELED A STICKER WORTH $200,000 TOWARD THE CONSTRUCTION OF A NEW HOME, REPORTS *U.S. NEWS & WORLD REPORT* (11/6/95).

WHAT WE GET OUT OF LIFE DEPENDS A LOT ON WHAT WE LOOK FOR. ARE WE MORE LIKELY TO SEE EACH EXPERIENCE AS TRASH OR A POTENTIAL TREASURE?[1]

A mountain mentioned in the Bible provides as accurate a picture of hope deferred as anything possibly could be. Wouldn't you know it would be a mountain! It looked like it stood for one thing, until God peeled off that which hid the treasure within. Its very name, Horeb, means desolation, a wasted place, barrenness, dryness[2]—all synonyms for hope deferred. It is the place where Moses ended up for much of the time during his

40-year exile, tending literal sheep instead of spiritual ones. There can be no more severe case of hope deferred than what Moses experienced, having lost his inheritance and, it seemed, his destiny. I know "it ain't over 'til it's over," but after disappearing for 40 years, a dream is usually over.

As God often does with obstacles, He transformed this mountain and harnessed its power and it became "the mountain of God" (Exod. 3:1). The events associated with it portray God's amazing ability to restore, heal and bring good from bad. *Horeb isn't always going to be horrible.* It is a real-life picture of the paradoxical nature of the kingdom of God—that good can come from bad, that we're strongest when we're weak and that life often flows out of death. The prophet Joel said, "Let the weak say, I am strong" (Joel 3:10, *KJV*). The Lord said to the apostle Paul, "My grace is sufficient for thee: for My strength is made perfect in weakness" (2 Cor. 12:9, *KJV*).

As in Joseph's story of betrayal, Satan has intended to destroy you through hope deferred; but God has plans— wonderful plans—for your hope-deferred heart disease. "'For I know the plans that I have for you,'" declares the Lord, "'plans for welfare and not for calamity to give you a future *and a hope*'" (Jer. 29:11, emphasis added). Mine the gold from this mountain; don't waste one tear caused by your pain.

God taught me this important truth a few years back while in a time of hope deferred, much of which had been caused by rejection and betrayal. In prayer I heard Him say to me, "I need for you to embrace the pain."

What a strange thing to hear from a loving Father who has great plans for my welfare and a future filled with hope. However, as a God who doesn't want to waste my pain but rather use it, He was encouraging me to allow it to do its work of purging, purifying and strengthening. I was not to embrace *betrayal* as something good; nor did God cause that betrayal; He doesn't produce sin in people's hearts. But I did need to embrace the pain so that it could do some positive things in me, much like the pain of an athlete in training produces good for the future. We often say, speaking of exercise, "No pain, no gain." Don't waste your hope-deferred pain.

Four significant events associated with Horeb, which we will explore in some detail, reveal many glorious pictures of God's redeeming grace and power. Learn the lessons well; for knowing His plan for our pain is one of the most important steps to faith for healing of hope deferred. Here are the four events, from which we will glean several significant insights:

- Moses experienced a renewed calling at Horeb (see Exod. 3—4).
- Israel received water from a rock at Horeb (see Exod.17).
- Moses met with God on Mount Horeb (see Exod. 19—33).
- Elijah overcame the spirit of Jezebel at Horeb (see 1 Kings 19).

Our first important lesson is that *at Horeb we learn to wait*. ("Duh!" I can almost hear some of you responding. But stay with me—waiting has a purpose and does come to an end.) After fleeing from Pharaoh and becoming an object lesson on hope deferred, Moses tended sheep around this mountain for 40 years before God reversed his situation and resurrected his destiny (see Exod. 3—4).

More waiting occurred at Horeb when Moses and the Israelites returned there a short time later (see Exod. 19—33). He and Joshua were called to this mountain by God, and for six days they did absolutely nothing but wait for God to speak to them and tell them why they were there. Six long days and nights of fasting and probably freezing, during which God said absolutely nothing (see Exod. 24:16). It must have seemed like a long time to Joshua; Moses probably just chuckled.

WE MUST LEARN TO WAIT WITHOUT WAVERING AND WE MUST RECOGNIZE THAT THE WAIT CAN BE A POSITIVE EXPERIENCE, FOR *LEARNING TO WAIT IS LEARNING TO PERSEVERE.*

Moses was then called into the cloud of God's presence (see v. 16), where he was with the Lord for the remaining 34 days. Joshua, however, was left alone on this barren, rocky mountain during that time, and we are told absolutely nothing about what he did or didn't do. We simply know that he waited on God and the man of God, Moses. Joshua was learning to wait—he would need the knowledge later.

There is no question about it: Horeb is a place of waiting. And nothing truer could be said than that waiting is associated with hope deferred. Many times we wait so long for our breakthrough, miracle or healing that it seems the only thing we experience is delay. We must learn, however, to wait without wavering—without allowing hope deferred to overcome us. And we must recognize that the wait can be a positive experience, for *learning to wait is learning to persevere*. In his book on hope, Rick DeVos, cofounder of Amway and owner of the Orlando Magic basketball team, says of persistence:

> Persistence is the single most important ingredient of success in life. When confronted with a failure or a disappointment, you have only two choices: You can give up, or you can persist. If I could pass on one character trait to young people in the world— one single quality that would help them achieve success in life—it would be persistence. It's more important than intellect, athletic ability, good looks or personal magnetism. Persistence comes from a deep place in the soul. It is a God-given compensation for what we lack in other areas of our life. Never underestimate its power.[3]

And so one of the great lessons of Horeb that all of us must learn if we are to overcome the tendency toward hope deferred is that the day of fruitfulness and fulfillment *will* come, *if we persevere.* Listen to the powerful words of Galatians 6:9 in the *Amplified* translation: "And let us not lose heart and grow weary and faint in acting nobly and doing right, for in due time and at the appointed season we shall reap, if we do not loosen and relax our courage and faint."

In the Greek the words "due time" (also rendered "appointed season") are *idios kairos*, which is a powerful phrase pregnant with hope seeds for us. "Time" is the word *kairos,* which means "right time; the opportune point of time at which something should be done."[4] *Idios* means "pertaining to self, i.e., one's own,"[5] denoting something owned or possessed by someone. The verse is communicating that though we will need to persevere in waiting, there is a well-timed answer owned by us.

You own a *kairos!*

"There is an appointed time for everything" (Eccles. 3:1), including "a time to heal" (v. 3). Acts 3:1-10 tells the exciting story of one man's *idios kairos*. Lame since birth, this man sat every day by the Temple gate to beg for money. So, interestingly, Jesus must have passed him by dozens of times and chosen not to heal him. Why? The answer is found here in Acts. God had reserved this miracle to be the first of the Early Church and, as a result, 5,000 people came to Christ (see Acts 4:4). *Sometimes God saves a miracle for a ripe harvest.* He may have more in mind for your breakthrough than just your breakthrough—your waiting may be harvest related. Without question, waiting is purposeful.

Such was the case with Hannah and Elizabeth, both barren women who asked God for a child (see 1 Sam. 1; Luke 1). In each case, the Lord answered with a son but waited for His timing because while they wanted a child, He needed a prophet. They owned a *kairos,* but God shared ownership; and His *kairos* involved not only their fulfillment, but also His eternal purposes.

And, as mentioned in chapter 1, Abraham was told by God in Genesis 18:10, "I will surely return to you at this time next year." "Time" is the Hebrew word *eth*, which is the counterpart of the Greek word *kairos.* Though Abraham and Sarah waited 25 years, they owned a right time, which was also the right time for God. His right time for our "Isaac" may not always be when we think it should be; but in our waiting we learn to persevere, and the higher purposes of God are established.

Another valuable lesson of Horeb is that our hearts must be exposed, *revealing to us where our trust really lies.* As such, it is a crucial part of our transformation. Moses, through his experience of hope deferred, was brought to the end of all self-confidence and to only a God-confidence. This work of God in his life, reaching its final stage at Horeb, is seen in the following Scripture passages:

> But Moses said to God, "Who am I, that I should go to Pharaoh, and that I should bring the sons of Israel out of Egypt?" (Exod. 3:11).

Then Moses said to the LORD, "Please, Lord, I have never been eloquent, neither recently nor in time past, nor since Thou hast spoken to Thy servant; for I am slow of speech and slow of tongue. . . . Please, Lord, now send the message by whomever Thou wilt" (Exod. 4:10-13).

Moses' self-confidence was brought to its lowest point here at Horeb. He was finally without pride or any belief in his own ability to perform the Lord's will. Sometimes God actually wants our hope to die, if our hope is in the wrong thing. He doesn't want us to be without confidence, but He does want us to be without self-confidence. Paul said in Romans 7:18, "For I know that nothing good dwells in me." Even Jesus realized He had to depend on the Father for His ability to accomplish His mission: "I can of mine own self do nothing" (John 5:30, *KJV*).

The weak level of trust among the entire nation of Israel was seen when they murmured and complained because they needed water (see Exod. 17:2). In their discomfort at Horeb, the Lord revealed their carnality and their lack of faith that He would come through. How often that is true with us! When we feel as though God hasn't come through for us in a certain area of our life, our level of trust is revealed. Rather than our words and actions confirming a solid trust in God, we often quarrel with others and test the Lord's patience.

Once more Israel's inability to trust God was exposed at Horeb. In Exodus 32, when Moses and Joshua were on the mountain with the Lord, Aaron and the Israelites built the golden calf idol. Verse 1 reveals that this was really a trust issue:

> Now when the people saw that Moses delayed to come down from the mountain, the people assembled about Aaron, and said to him, "Come, *make us a god who will go before us;* as for this Moses, the man who brought us up from the land of Egypt, we do not know what has become of him" (Exod. 32:1, emphasis added).

The Israelites had become convinced that Moses and Joshua were never coming off of Horeb. "Moses is gone, along with his God," they were saying, "and we need another god to care for us." Still defiled by the idolatry of Egypt, they were not able in this time of testing to anchor their faith in the Lord.

Horeb—the difficult times of barrenness and desolation when hope deferred creeps in—exposes our hearts and reveals to us where our trust lies. When our faith is in the wrong place, God's desire is always to deliver us from our error and bring transformation, as seen in the following testimony:

> Mike Holmgren was all-American quarterback in high school, played for UCLA in college, and dreamed of a career in the NFL. His excitement was unbounded when the St. Louis Cardinals drafted

him; but he was cut during the preseason. Then the New York Jets considered him as Joe Namath's backup but later went with another player.

[Mike says] *"I was crushed. All that had mattered to me was playing pro football, and now that would never happen. I felt like a failure."*

Returning home, Mike retreated to his bedroom in depression and there found his old dust-covered Bible. He had become a Christian at age 11, but in his intense pursuit of football had forgotten the Lord. As he thumbed through the Bible, Proverbs 3:5-6 caught his attention, and Mike recommitted his life to Jesus Christ.

Shortly afterward, Mike began coaching at his high school alma mater and has been coaching ever since, becoming one of the most successful NFL coaches in America.

"Win or lose," Mike says, "I now realize what really matters: It's not the Super Bowl rings—it's the crown of eternal life that Jesus Christ has won for us through His victory on the cross."[6]

Like Mike Holmgren, make sure your hope and trust are in the right place—not in a career, your abilities or what others believe about you, but in the Lord.

The next truth we learn at the place of desolation—Horeb—is *the power of God's word.* I know we can always hear God speaking to us through the Scriptures, but there are times when God seems to be very silent about our situation. I can assure you of this, however: If we persevere in the Horeb times, there will come a point when God will speak. His perspective will be given to us concerning our situation, and His redemptive plan in it all will be seen.

In 1 Kings 19, Elijah, after his battle with the prophets of Baal and his stand against Ahab and Jezebel, somehow found himself discouraged and overcome, I believe, not by Jezebel herself, but by the spirit of Jezebel. He was isolated, depressed, weary and afraid, and he had become so discouraged that he wanted to die (see 1 Kings 19:4). He was in a hope-deferred mess and had a very sick heart. God's solution was to send him "to Horeb, the mountain of God" (1 Kings 19:8).

There Elijah found himself in a cave. Many scholars believe this was the same cave, or cleft, that Moses was in when God passed before (*abar*) him (see Exod. 33:19-23). And the same thing occurred with Elijah as with Moses: "The LORD was passing by [*abar*]" (1 Kings 19:11).

This word *abar* means "to cross over or into; to pass by or into."[7] Basically it means moving from one place to another. Sometimes *abar* is a very generic word for passing into or crossing over one place to another, and it is used this way hundreds of times in the Old Testament. Other times the passing into or crossing over is a very significant, meaningful and life-changing experience.

Interestingly enough, because *abar* is a transition word, it also means "to penetrate,"[8] as in penetrating territory or even the human heart. And, not trying to be overly dramatic or graphic, it is indeed a word used in the physical relationship of a husband and wife that results in pregnancy. Yes, the word can mean "to impregnate."[9] An *abar* experience with God can be so significant that we find ourselves pregnant with a new nature, mission, calling or understanding.

God spoke at Horeb in "the sound of a gentle whisper" (1 Kings 19:12, *TLB*), He made Elijah pregnant with the seed of His word. He was impregnated with the ability to impart a double-portion anointing to Elisha and an anointing to Jehu and Hazael, who would finish the work of disposing of Ahab and Jezebel.

Think about it. At the time when Elijah felt the weakest, God came to him and spoke a word—and Elijah found himself pregnant with the power of multiplication. He was able to give a double portion of the anointing in him to Elisha. And Jehu, after being anointed by him, finished the job of

IN THE TIMES WHEN GOD HAS BEEN SILENT AND WE SEEM TO BE LIVING IN BARRENNESS, EVENTUALLY HE WILL SPEAK, AND REMEMBER, HOPE OFTEN COMES IN A WHISPER.

overthrowing evil Ahab and Jezebel, a job that Elijah could only begin. *At Horeb, out of Elijah's weakness flowed strength.*

God can do this for us as well. At Horeb, in our place of hope deferred, in the times when God has been silent and we seem to be living in barrenness, eventually He will speak. When He does, we become pregnant with what we need in order to finish our race. In John 6:63, Jesus states, "The words that I have spoken to you are spirit and are life." When we hear God speak to us, as it was with Elijah, the life in His words becomes life in us.

And remember, hope often comes in a whisper.

Horeb also represents newness. God can metamorphose the pain of hope deferred into such a transforming power that Horeb, as paradoxically as it sounds, becomes *a place of new beginnings.* It was here that Moses' calling was restored in Exodus 3—4. He thought his destiny was lost forever. And talk about irony, no place could have been a more accurate picture of his life story than this very mountain where he worked tending sheep. Its very name, Horeb, meaning "desolation and barrenness," must have been a constant reminder to Moses of his hope deferred, adding insult to injury: "Not only is my life Horeb, but I work there."

Moses was so filled with hopelessness that in these two chapters God never was really able to bring him to a place of accepting his renewed calling. Moses consistently tried to tell the Lord that he was not qualified and did not want to do it. God finally had to essentially say to him, "I've heard enough! You are going to do this" (see Exod. 4:14-17). God cares more about our destinies than we do!

When Timothy's spiritual father, Paul, had to get him restarted, he told Timothy to "kindle afresh" his gifts (2 Tim. 1:6). The word for "kindle afresh" is *anazoporeo*, which is composed of three Greek words: *Ana* means "again"; *zo* traces back to *zao*, from which we get the concept of being alive; and *pureo* is from *pur*, meaning "fire or lighting." The point is to "get the fire alive again" or to "get the life in you burning again."

"Let your gifts live again!" he said to Timothy. "Burn with passion!"

Paul reminded Timothy that he had been called "with a holy calling . . . according to His own purpose and grace" (2 Tim. 1:9). "Purpose" is the word *prothesis*, which means setting forth the purpose of a thing (*thesis*) in advance (*pro*). God has a destiny for us and He is committed to it. He is the beginning and the end and, when necessary, a new beginning in between.

"Prosthesis" is an English word we get from *prothesis*. It is an artificial part of the human body (such as an arm, a leg or even teeth) built to restore purpose to that part of the body. Paul was saying to his spiritual son Timothy, "He made you with a purpose, and when that seems to have been lost, He can recreate it, restoring your purpose."

Horeb, as much as any other place, illustrates the fact that new beginnings are brought forth from the place of desolation and hope-deferred pain. There we discover that

God is bigger—not only bigger than our enemies but also bigger than our mistakes, sins, shortcomings and fears. As such, Horeb becomes a wonderful place of new beginnings.

A dear friend and powerful intercessor, who has ministered all over the world, experienced a fresh start at Horeb many years ago. Listen to Bobbye Byerly's testimony of the transforming power of God:

> There's no pretty way to say it. I was 28 years old and miserable. My marriage was falling apart after 10 years. We had three small sons and I'd lost two babies in miscarriages. My semi-invalid mother-in-law, Maggie, lived with us and required considerable care. My father had just died, and I was flying from New Jersey to Texas for his funeral. I had lost the capacity to love and couldn't overcome the stress in my life. I felt as if I were living with a bag over my head and couldn't breathe.
>
> As I traveled alone to my father's funeral, a Japanese man seated next to me on the plane initiated conversation and eventually asked, "Do you know my Jesus?"
>
> What a question to ask *me!* I was an American woman who had always gone to church. I turned away, contemplating the turn of events in my life. I would soon see my mother, who had just been released from another stay in a mental hospital, as well as other family members, many of whom had

helped raise my siblings and me during my mom's numerous hospitalizations. During the next few days, the Japanese traveler's question haunted me. *Did I know Jesus?*

After I returned home, I began to seek counsel from my pastor. We had agreed to meet for six sessions starting in mid-April, and I had told him about my plan to take the boys and leave my husband in June. On June 8, I entered the pastor's office for my last counseling session. He had attempted to reveal truth to me during our previous meetings, but I was living in darkness, unable to receive light.

Suddenly, without thinking about it, I blurted out, "A man seated next to me on the plane as I was flying to Daddy's funeral asked me if I knew Jesus. The question is haunting me. Do you think I know Jesus?"

My pastor must have been shocked. I was a Sunday School teacher and president of the women's group at our church. Jim and I were both active in our congregation, and on the surface our lives looked good. But I knew I was like the "whitewashed tombs" Jesus described in Matthew 23:27— beautiful on the outside, but inside full of dead men's bones and uncleanness.

I can't fully explain what happened in the next few moments after my question, but the light of God's glory supernaturally filled the pastor's office.

I suddenly saw myself a sinner in need of a Savior and began crying out to Him. The Lord miraculously set me free of fear and bitterness, while His love and grace enveloped me. I picked up a Bible and it opened to Deuteronomy 30:19-20. I stood up and boldly declared, "I choose life!"

I left that room a transformed woman. Even the world around me seemed to be bursting forth in technicolor. I realized I had been in such darkness that I had not seen spring arrive. When I reached the house, I raced up to my mother-in-law's room, excited to tell someone what had happened to me. As I shared with her, God's miraculous love healed us both—her of a cardiovascular infirmity which had made her semi-invalid for nine years, and me of debilitating resentment and bitterness. My marriage began afresh, too, as I fell in love again with the special guy I had married. God's amazing grace transformed our lives.[10]

As long as Jesus lives, there is always hope. The psalmist said we *pass through* the valley of Baca (weeping), not that it is our permanent resting place (see Ps. 84:6).

I know you have waited, some of you a long time; but like Bobbye, you do own a *kairos*. Anchor your trust in the Lord. He is coming to you with an *abar* word, making you pregnant with hope and a new beginning.

CHAPTER 6

HOREB,
THE HOLY PLACE

Billy Graham had a friend who during the Depression lost his job, a fortune, a wife and a home. But this man tenaciously held to his faith—the only thing he had left. One day he stopped to watch some men doing stonework on a huge church. One of them was chiseling a triangular piece of stone. "What are you going to do with that?" asked his friend. The workman said, "See that little opening away up there near the spire? Well, I'm shaping this down here, so it will fit in up there."

Tears filled his eyes as he walked away, for it seemed that God had spoken through the workman to explain his ordeal through which he was passing, "I'm shaping you down here so you'll fit in up there."[1]

Yes, God is shaping us—and not just for "up there." God is also shaping us for our future down here. In the process, He doesn't intend to waste one difficult day spent at Horeb.

In fact, *God's tools—His provision for our future—are given to us at Horeb*. We will leave there better equipped than when we came. At this mountain, God asked Moses, "What is that in your hand?" (Exod. 4:2). Moses held a simple staff that he used for walking and tending his sheep. The Hebrew word for "staff" is *matteh*,[2] which is also the word for "scepter." Moses' scepter was just a crooked, knobby, dead piece of wood found and shaped on the mountain of desolation; but the staff of Horeb became "the staff of God" (Exod. 4:20).

God was not looking for a polished, gold-plated, gem-studded scepter of Egypt. He was saying to Moses, "I took from you the golden scepter of Egypt and instead gave you one from Horeb that symbolizes brokenness, meekness and no confidence in the flesh. It has indeed been a staff of hope-deferred desolation, but I am transforming it into My staff. I am turning your brokenness into strength and your meekness into confidence in Me. Because this has occurred, I can give you great authority." In Exodus 4:17 God declared, "Take this staff in your hand so you can perform miraculous signs *with it*" (*NIV*, emphasis added).

With that ugly staff of Horeb—representing broken-ness, meekness and confidence in God alone—Moses judged nations, parted seas, brought forth water from a rock and held it high on a mountaintop, which caused victory over the enemies of God. He didn't accomplish these feats with a staff representing his strength but with one that represent-ed his weakness. It is our brokenness that allows Him to place His authority in us. What a precious truth!

At Horeb the tools for our future—that which we need in order to accomplish His purposes for our lives—are put in our hands. The authority and anointing necessary to defeat enemy strongholds are often given at Horeb. After the rock of Horeb was smitten, the Amalekites attacked Israel (see Exod. 17). Moses was instructed to go up onto the mountain with the staff of Horeb, "the staff of God," and hold it up over the battlefield. Through the authority represented by this rod of God, Joshua defeated the enemy. What a powerful picture for us of a Horeb-produced weapon conquering our enemies! Hope-deferred places can become weapon factories.

This concept is amply illustrated by the story of a girl named Little Annie. Although she didn't know it at the time, her place of utter hopelessness provided the necessary tools for her future:

> In an asylum that dealt with severely mentally retarded and disturbed individuals was a girl called Little Annie. Totally unresponsive to the staff's many attempts to help her, she was finally confined to a cell in the basement of the asylum and given up as hopeless.
>
> One of the workers, however, spent her lunch hours in front of Little Annie's cell, reading to her and praying that God would free her from her prison of silence. Day after day, this woman came to Little Annie's door, but the little girl made no response.
>
> Then, many months later, the little girl began to speak and, amazingly, within two years she was

told that she could leave the asylum and enjoy a normal life. But Little Annie chose not to leave, and instead stayed on to work with other patients.

Nearly half a century later, at a special ceremony to honor her life, Helen Keller was asked to what she would attribute her success at overcoming her handicaps. She replied, "If it hadn't been for Ann Sullivan, I wouldn't be here today."

Ann Sullivan, who tenaciously loved and believed in an incorrigible blind and deaf girl named Helen Keller, was Little Annie.[3]

Annie's experiences in the asylum equipped her to bring transformation to Helen Keller's world. What has He put in your hands through your place of brokenness? If you look, you will find there is now a strength and authority you possess only because you spent time at Horeb.

At Horeb—the dry, difficult place that so often breeds hope deferred—*new revelations of God are given,* as seen in the following examples:

- Moses received the revelation of God as "I AM THAT I AM" (Exod. 3:14, *KJV*).
- Israel received the revelation that God is *Jehovah Nissi,* the Lord our Banner and Victory, the One who fights our battles for us (see Exod. 17:15).
- The Lord came to Moses, showing him His goodness and glory (see Exod. 33:19-23).

- After the episode with the golden calf, a new revelation of God's mercy and grace was seen when, through Moses' intercession, the Lord spared the nation and did not destroy all of them (see Exod. 32:11-14). Though there was judgment, there was also mercy.

I love Exodus 19:17, which states, "And Moses brought the people out of the camp *to meet God*, and they stood at the foot of the mountain" (emphasis added). Stand at the bottom of Desolation Mountain and meet with God! What a thought! Yes, we can meet God at Horeb. Like Moses at the burning bush and all of Israel at the foot of the mountain, we encounter God in new ways at Horeb. And when we meet with Him, new revelations of His nature and of His Father heart come forth.

In the previous chapter we spoke of Elijah's visit to Horeb, after he had been overcome by hope deferred and the spirit of Jezebel. He was in such a deep place of fear and depression that he asked God to take his life. The Lord led him to Horeb, where He placed Elijah in a cave and met with him. The same word *abar* is used to describe both Moses' and Elijah's visitations (when God "passed by") on the mountain. And as we said previously, many scholars believe it was the same cleft of the rock, or cave, that Moses and Elijah were in when they were visited with the glory of the Lord (compare Exod. 33:22 and 1 Kings 19:11). Also, some of the same manifestations of God's presence (thunder, fire, etc.) that happened with Moses occurred with Elijah.

What might the Lord have been saying to Elijah through all these "sames"—mountain, cave, *abar* and manifestations? What Horeb revelation was He bringing forth? I believe it was this: At Horeb, *the God of history becomes the God of today*. When we speak of new revelations of God, one of the most important revelations is that He is the same yesterday, today and forever (see Heb. 13:8). The God of our fathers must become our God. The God we've heard about must become the One we've experienced. We can't really hope in God until we have a revelation of Him as "the God of hope" (Rom. 15:13).

Jacob is a wonderful picture of this as well. As remarkable as it seems, until his experience at Penuel when he was 40 years old, you will never find him calling God "his God." And you will never find others speaking to Jacob and referring to God as "Jacob's God." In Genesis 31:5, 31:42 and 32:9, Jacob calls Him "the God of my father." The Lord Himself spoke to Jacob in Genesis 26:24 and 28:13 saying, "I am the God of your father." Even Laban, his father-in-law, in Genesis 31:29 refers to God as "the God of your father."

But after Jacob was broken and poured out—sounds like Horeb to me—he built an altar and called it El-Elohe-Israel, which means "God, the God of Israel" (see Gen. 33:20). When he named this altar, the Israel he was referring to was not a race of people, nor was it a land. He was talking about himself—he who had just had his name changed from Jacob to Israel (see Gen. 32:28). When he wrote "God, the God of Israel" on the altar, he was declaring, "He is not just the God of my father or my grandfather. He is *my* God!" That is incredible. Don't waste your Horeb hope-deferred experience. Allow it to introduce you to a facet of our many-faceted God.

The Lord wants you to receive this revelation at Horeb, in your place of hope deferred. It's interesting that there are times when God called Himself by a certain name, i.e., I AM THAT I AM, and there are other times in Scripture when an individual gave Him a name, as Jacob did. Moses also gave Him one: "the Lord our Banner." Go ahead and give him a personal name, "El-Elohe-Susan, or -Tom, or -Debra." He must become all that He is *to you*.

God can be a healer, a savior and a thousand other things yet not be any of them to you. He can be the God of hope and not be yours—He can be known about and yet not be known; He can be all things *in* you but not all things *to* you. The God of history must become *your* God today.

It is also in the difficult place—Horeb—that *His plans and pattern for our future are revealed*. On this very mountain Moses received the plans for the Tabernacle, the Ark of the Covenant, the Feasts and even the laws of this new nation. God chose this mountain to give Moses the blueprint for the future of Israel. As we've already said, Horeb is a place of great revelation; and a part of that revelation involves our future. You can leave Horeb—the mountain of hope deferred, the place of sick hearts—not only with a healed heart but also with plans for your destiny and a revelation of the future! Your past will finally make sense—as will your future.

Many times we cannot understand our past until He reveals our future. Concerning Joseph's journey through hope deferred—slavery, a prison in Egypt and finally to the throne—God essentially said to him, "Your brothers meant this to *dislocate* you. I meant it to *relocate* you." Only on the other side of hope deferred did this revelation come. His brothers wanted to destroy the man, but God wanted to preserve a nation.

Perhaps Satan has intended to make you an outcast, but God wants to use your experience to give you a love for outcasts. Maybe Satan's intention was to rob you of a loved one, but God wants to use you to bring healing to those who have lost loved ones. There are always two plans for our difficult times—God's and Satan's. Often it is not until we come through to the other side of our

OFTEN IT IS NOT UNTIL WE COME THROUGH TO THE OTHER SIDE OF OUR PAIN, HOPELESSNESS AND DESPAIR THAT GOD'S REDEMPTIVE PLAN FOR SATAN'S EVIL IS REVEALED.

pain, hopelessness and despair that God's redemptive plan for Satan's evil is revealed.

It is doubtful that Susanna Wesley, in the midst of horrible circumstances, could have ever imagined the incredible purpose God had for two of her children:

> Susanna Annesley was born in 1669, the last of 25 children. Married to Samuel Wesley, she gave birth to 19 children, nine of whom died in infancy. Her life was turbulent, frequently unhappy and filled with trials. Samuel was often gone from home, leaving her alone and almost penniless to care for the family. Unable to properly manage his small salary, he was put in debtor's prison for a time. They disagreed on many points in both politics and religion, resulting in further separations and conflicts. They lived in impoverished circumstances; at one point their home burned to the ground. Susanna suffered from many illnesses and was often bed-ridden, requiring household help. Between 1697 and 1701, Susanna gave birth to five babies, including twins, all of whom died. Three children later, in 1705, an exhausted nursemaid rolled over onto the newest baby and suffocated it. Many of her children who did live were so errant that they caused her considerable grief.
>
> Yet her sons John and Charles became two of the greatest evangelists of all time, and their ministry shook the world.[4]

Your Horeb may seem so devastating that you can't see how anything good could possibly come from it. But God does have a plan, and He will bring about His redemptive purposes in your life. Hope!

Another wonderful work produced by the Holy Spirit at Horeb is *a fresh flow of His river—of power, anointing and fruitfulness—to us*. It was at this mountain, in Exodus 17:6, that Israel was in desperate need of water, and God brought it forth from a rock. First Corinthians 10:4 says that rock pictured Christ. He is "the rock at Horeb" (Exod. 17:6). When it doesn't look like there is water at Horeb—the dry place of difficulty, despair and desolation—all the same, it is there. Thirsty people find water at Horeb.

This smitten rock is also a picture of the crucifixion, when Christ our Rock was smitten for us and the fountain of life flowed. All that the Cross represents—forgiveness of sin, healing of broken hearts, eternal life—is pictured by this event. It is fair to say that not just in spite of Horeb, not just when we get away from Horeb, but *out of* Horeb flows a river of life. God redeems the horrible, dry place and transforms it into a place from which the river of life flows. Isaiah speaks of rivers in the desert (see Isa. 43:19-20). Wanting a river in the desert sounds to me like Abraham's hoping against hope. Go ahead, though, because we serve an amazing God.

You can leave hope deferred with a greater dimension of the power and anointing of the Holy Spirit—the river of God—as shown in the following story:

Poor health haunted Dr. A. B. Simpson, and a physician told him he would never live to be 40. This diagnosis underscored the physical helplessness the minister knew only too well. Preaching was an agonizing effort. Walking was painful, and climbing even a slight elevation brought on a suffocating agony of breathlessness.

In desperation, sick in body and despairing in spirit, Dr. Simpson went to his Bible. He became convinced that Jesus intended healing to be part of the redemption of man's total being. He prayed, asking Christ to fulfill all the needs of his body, until his life's work was done. Every fiber in him tingled with the sense of God's presence.

During the first three years after this healing, he preached more than a thousand sermons, conducting sometimes as many as 20 meetings in one week. For the rest of his life, he was noted for the amazing volume of his sermonic, pastoral and literary work.

Simpson lived to be 76, but his work has lived after him. The Christian and Missionary Alliance, which he founded, is still a potent spiritual force today; his books are still being published and are blessing millions of people.[5]

At his place of hope deferred, Dr. Simpson drank of the river of life, and not only was he revived but also streams from that fountain are still flowing and impacting lives today.

Finally, the desolate place *becomes the holy place.* Moses was told at Horeb, "Remove your sandals from your feet, for the place on which you are standing is holy ground" (Exod. 3:5). Later, the Lord told Moses the mountain was so holy that if any person or animal touched it, they would die:

And you shall set bounds for the people all around, saying, "Beware that you do not go up on the mountain or touch the border of it; whoever touches the mountain shall surely be put to death. No hand shall touch him, but he shall surely be stoned or shot through; whether beast or man, he shall not live" (Exod. 19:12-13).

GOD TAKES THE DIFFICULT PLACES AND THROUGH HIS INCREDIBLE WISDOM AND POWER TRANSFORMS THEM INTO SOMETHING GOOD.

The Horeb-ble place became the holy place. God had told Moses that he would come back to "this mountain" and worship God (see Exod. 3:12). Not "you shall come back to this awful place"; not "you shall come back to this mountain and curse it." No, they were to go back to this place, *which was now holy,* and worship.

I know that in the deep, dark night of the soul, hope seems impossible. And it is, really. It's just that our God does the impossible. He takes the difficult places—the things that brought about our hope deferred—and through His incredible wisdom and power transforms them into something good. So good, in fact, that later we can actually return to that place and worship Him, saying, "God, I don't know how You did it, but in this difficult place You proved Yourself faithful and brought life to me. I worship You."

Moses probably said, "For 40 years I thought this place was horrible. Now I realize it's holy." Some of the most dramatic encounters and visitations humanity has ever experienced with God, Moses had on this mountain called "desolation." Yes, out of our brokenness, out of our place of pain, God knows how to bring healing and make it a place of worship.

At the Royal Palace of Tehran, in Iran, you can see one of the most beautiful mosaic works in the world. The ceilings and walls flash like diamonds in multifaceted reflections.

Originally, when the palace was designed, the architect specified huge sheets of mirrors on the walls. When the first shipment arrived from Paris, they found to their horror that the mirrors were shattered. The contractor threw them in the trash and brought the sad news to the architect.

Amazingly, the architect ordered all of the broken pieces collected, then smashed them into tiny pieces and glued them to the walls to become a mosaic of silvery, shimmering, mirrored bits of glass.

Broken to become beautiful! It's possible to turn your scars into stars. It's possible to be better because of the brokenness. It is extremely rare to find in the great museums of the world objects of antiquity that are unbroken. Indeed some of the most precious pieces in the world are only fragments that remain a hallowed reminder of a glorious past. [6]

We may feel that our lives have been hopelessly destroyed; but God doesn't see it that way. He intends to form those broken pieces into something exquisitely wonderful. Never underestimate God's power to repair and restore.

C H A P T E R   7

EXPECT!

FOR THERE IS HOPE FOR A TREE, WHEN IT IS CUT DOWN, THAT IT WILL SPROUT AGAIN, AND ITS SHOOTS WILL NOT FAIL. THOUGH ITS ROOTS GROW OLD IN THE GROUND, AND ITS STUMP DIES IN THE DRY SOIL, AT THE SCENT OF WATER IT WILL FLOURISH AND PUT FORTH SPRIGS LIKE A PLANT (JOB 14:7-9).

Hope has now become a reality to you. Even though you may have felt like a tree totally destroyed and cut down, you can now smell water—the water of the Spirit of God—and you have hope.

You're going to sing again.

You're going to dance again.

You are going to live.

You are going to climb out of the debris and crow.

By the grace of God and the power of the Holy Spirit, you're going to get busy livin'! You will be like the woman in Mark's gospel, who refused to give up:

And a woman who had had a hemorrhage for twelve years, and had endured much at the hands of many physicians, and had spent all that she had and was not helped at all, but rather had grown worse, after hearing about Jesus, came up in the crowd behind Him, and touched His cloak (Mark 5:25-27).

This woman had suffered an ongoing, incurable condition for many years. She was, no doubt, weak from the continual drain on her system. Many doctors—yes, the passage says "many"—had put her through numerous difficult experiences. She had exhausted all of her resources yet had grown worse. There was no hope, but she still hoped anyway.

Even though the Law of Moses forbade anyone in her "unclean" condition to touch others, she wasn't going to miss her time of healing. She had more faith in Jesus' power to heal her than she had in her ability to defile Him. "I'm going to touch Him," she determined. "I don't care how crowded it is, how far away He is from me or how many hundreds of people are between us. I don't care who

DEEP WITHIN YOU THERE IS A SPIRIT OF FAITH, JUST WAITING TO BE RESURRECTED. GET TO HIM! WHATEVER IT TAKES, TOUCH HIM. CRAWL IF YOU HAVE TO, BUT GET TO HIM.

thinks I am breaking the Law of Moses by touching others and Him. Even if I have to crawl, reach out and just touch the hem of His garment, *I am going to get to Jesus and receive my healing.*"

Don't you love her indomitable spirit? That's what I call dancing. That's hope!

And you're going to do that! Deep within you there is a spirit of faith, just waiting to be resurrected. Get to Him! Whatever it takes, touch Him. Crawl if you have to, but get to Him. Even if you have spent all that you have, and the doctors, therapists, friends and anyone else say there's no hope for you, hope anyway! Push through the fear, pain, confusion and the mob of circumstances that stand in your way—and *get to Jesus.* This is a choice you must make.

In this chapter I want to encourage your faith by planting specific seeds in you—hope seeds, faith seeds. This chapter is simply a declaration of biblical promises that God wants to fulfill in your life, without illustrations or stories. I urge and encourage you, even challenge you, to stir yourself up by beginning to expect these things. Make a conscious choice to believe that they are going to happen. You will partake of hope fulfilled.

Several months ago the Lord quickened Isaiah 59 and 60 to my heart. I felt strongly that it was a word for the Body of Christ in this season. Subsequently, I received a letter from my friend Chuck Pierce, who said exactly the same thing. He even had a list of things to begin to expect that was very similar to what God had showed me through this passage of Scripture. I know this is a word from the Lord for you. Allow these expectations to encourage your faith. As you take hold of them and apply them in your life, you will reap a bountiful harvest of good fruit.

Expect the Zeal of the Lord to Come to You with Justice, Salvation and an Outpouring of His Holy Spirit

Isaiah 59:15-21 shows the intensity with which God desires to bring deliverance. He is zealous for you. Justice and salvation (wholeness) are coming to your life as a holy invasion. His Spirit will be poured out upon you.

While in prayer several months ago, I saw the Lord coming to this nation in a whirlwind with a terrifying zeal and intensity in His eyes. His Spirit swept across America bringing revival to college campuses, high schools, middle schools and grade schools. Miracles, signs and wonders began to occur, including instantaneous deliverances by the power of God. I saw thousands of young people coming to Christ.

True revival is near. The Lord is coming with great zeal. Expect salvation to come to your offspring (Isa. 59:21; 60:4). Expect the prodigals to come home. Expect those who are rebellious, addicted, into perversions and bound by all manner of sin to be delivered. Salvation is coming to your household. Expect it!

Expect the Glory of the Lord to Come to and upon You

Isaiah 60:1 in the *Amplified* declares: "Arise [from the depression and prostration in which circumstances have kept you—rise to a new life!] Shine (be radiant with the glory of the Lord), for your light has come, and the glory of the Lord has risen upon you!"

The Hebrew word for glory has the meaning of something that is heavy or weighty. The Greek concept is to recognize someone or something for who or what it really is. Expect the weighty, heavy glory of God to invade your life, devastate your enemies and deliver you from your depression and fear. Believe it! Expect Him to be recognized in your life—His glory is coming to you.

Expect Light to Shine on Your Path

Isaiah 60:2-3 communicates that light will overcome darkness. Look for the light of understanding to come where you have been confused. As you read and meditate on Scripture, expect to receive revelation. The light of God that grows brighter and brighter until the full day is going to shine on your path (see Prov. 4:18). No longer will you walk in the darkness of hope deferred, groping to find your way. You are coming into a season of light. Expect it.

Expect His Presence to Be Manifested in Your Life in a New Way

Isaiah 60:2 says that "the LORD will rise upon you." If you have grown cold or lukewarm in your walk with God, expect His presence to awaken you to a new season of intimacy. Expect a fresh passion for the Lord to be ignited within you. Anticipate visitations from Him in the night hours. In your quiet times with Him, look for the reality of who He is to explode off the pages of His Word. Expect His presence to overwhelm you.

Expect New Vision to Come to You

Isaiah 60:4 in the *Moffat* translation states: "Look around you, look! How all are flocking in, your sons from far away, your daughters carried on the arm!" This is a day for renewed vision. If you, like Moses and Abraham, have suffered from hope deferred and lost your vision, expect new vision to explode in you. Look! It is not a time for retreat, apathy, hopelessness or stagnation. Take hold of a fresh ability to see ahead as never before.

Isaiah was prophesying future events, challenging them to see *by faith.* Jesus said in John 4:35, "Lift up your eyes, and look on the fields, that they are white for harvest." He was telling them to look by faith. Elijah said he heard the "sound of abundance of rain" before there was ever a cloud in the sky (1 Kings 18:41, *KJV*). Begin to see with the eyes of faith in this new season. Stir up your expectations—new vision is about to burst forth!

Expect New Joy to Rise Up in You

"Then you shall see and be radiant, and your heart shall thrill and tremble with joy [at the glorious deliverance] and be enlarged" (Isa. 60:5, *Amplified*). The Hebrew word translated "thrill" means to "tremble or palpitate." You are going to be so excited as hope wells up within you that your heart is going to race! Your diseased heart is being healed to such an extent that it will have the capacity to rejoice. Expect the joy of the Lord to become your strength (see Neh. 8:10). Deliverance is coming to you, and instead of oppression you will have joy. You are being healed of hope deferred, and joy is going to overwhelm you. Expect it!

Expect Abundant Provision

Isaiah 60:5-7 tell of the coming of bountiful supplies. Expect those supplies in your life! God wants to meet your every need according to His riches in glory in Christ Jesus (see Phil. 4:19). Expect poverty to break off of you and the lack in which you have previously walked to be turned into a place of more than enough. Anticipate the arrival of abundance. Expect God's tools, provisions and resources to be released to you in great measure.

Expect the Favor of the Lord to Come to You

Isaiah 60:10 says, "In My favor I have had compassion on you." Expect favor wherever you are—in your job, family, church, marriage, business endeavors, community—every place you go. Jesus came "to proclaim the favorable year of the Lord" (Luke 4:19). Look for His favor to open doors for you, to bring the contacts that you need and to prepare the way before you. Expect the favor of the Lord in all of your relationships.

The next list of "expects" is gleaned from Peter's hope-deferred jail time we read about in Acts 12. This was a time of tremendous prosperity, as well as great persecution, in the

Early Church. Wonderful things were happening spiritually, and yet Herod had begun to attack them. He had killed James, the brother of John, and then arrested Peter, putting him into prison and planning to execute him as well. The Church prayed fervently for Peter's release, and he had a dramatic visitation from an angel who delivered him from prison. Here are several expectations taken from this chapter. I encourage you to read all of it when possible, as I will only be quoting small portions.

Expect Angelic Visitations

"And behold, an angel of the Lord suddenly appeared" (Acts 12:7). I don't necessarily mean you will see angels, although some of you may; but expect them to fulfill in your life what the Scriptures say they do. Expect angelic protection. Believe that they will bear you up in their arms, protecting you (see Ps. 91:11-12). Anticipate their encampment round about you (see Ps. 34:7). Look for angelic visits to bring healing and provision into your life. And, yes, expect them to invade your prison of hope-deferred bondage and deliver you from it. Expect your mountain of Horeb to rumble and shake with the presence of God and angelic visitors.

Expect a Light to Shine in Your Prison

"And a light shone in the cell" (Acts 12:7). Expect your night to give way to the dawn. I recently heard a good friend, Pastor Lon Stokes, share from this passage. He connected it to Genesis and the significance of God beginning each day of

Creation with darkness. The process of God always involves night. In fact, spiritual birthing begins at night. Expect the Holy Spirit to hover over the darkness of your hope-deferred night and to create a new day of hope, just as He did in Genesis 1. Expect a light to shine in your cell of despair, transforming your surroundings. Expect the light of hope to break forth as the dawn!

Expect Your Chains to Fall Off

Scripture says of Peter, "And his chains fell off his hands" (Acts 12:7). You have the right to freedom. Hope deferred is beginning to yield to victory. This is a day of breakthrough. Believe it. If you've been enslaved to sin, this is your hour to be free. If you've been held captive by oppression, discouragement and depression, this is your point of release. If you've been imprisoned with disease, this is your time to be healed. If you've been bound with hopelessness, this is your day to hope. Expect your chains to fall off! The demoniacs in Matthew 8:28-32 were hopelessly bound in an impossible condition, yet Jesus delivered them in a moment. Expect breakthrough. Your *idios kairos*—the time that you own—is here. Expect it!

Expect Your Prison Doors to Open

"Peter followed him out of the prison" (Acts 12:9, *NIV*). You are going to be free. Jesus came to release you from the prison of hope deferred. Luke 4:18 states, "He has sent me to proclaim freedom for the prisoners" (*NIV*). You are walking out of the captivity that has kept you bound and into a new place of freedom. Tell your heart to start beating again. It's time to get busy livin'!

Expect Gates to Open

"They came to the iron gate that leads into the city, which opened for them by itself" (Acts 12:10). Gates refer to authority. Expect the authority of the Lord to be released into your life. You will possess the gate of your enemy (see Gen. 22:17). Gates will open to the Lord (see Ps. 24:7-9). The gates of hell will no longer prevail against you (see Matt. 16:18). The King of Glory is coming into your city, your home, your family and your life. Expect the gate of hope to open!

Expect Your Enemies to Fall

"And immediately an angel of the Lord struck him" (Acts 12:23). Herod, who had thrown Peter in jail, was stricken and died. Of course, this expectation does not refer to people but to the enemies of your soul. The strongholds associated with hope deferred in your life will come down. The enemies that have tried to imprison you are going to be defeated. God's enemies—those who oppose the gospel and the believer—will fall. "Let God arise, let His enemies be scattered; and let those who hate Him flee before Him" (Ps. 68:1).

Expect the Word of the Lord to Grow and Be Multiplied

"But the word of God grew and multiplied" (Acts 12:24, *KJV*).

Expect the Word of the Lord to prosper in you. Expect the Word of the Lord over your city and nation to increase and be fulfilled. Expect every promise from Scripture to come to pass in your life. Hope in God's Word. Expect it to grow and multiply. "The LORD will command His lovingkindness in the daytime; and His song will be with [you] in the night" (Ps. 42:8). The God of hope will fill you with all joy and peace in believing and you will abound in hope (see Rom. 15:13)!

A life full of hope is your destiny. Don't settle for anything less. Remember Bartimaeus in Mark 10? He was determined to receive his sight. When he knew his healing was within range, this man shouted out, "Jesus, Son of David, have mercy on me!" (v. 47). People around him insisted that he be quiet, but he didn't care about what people were saying to him. Nothing was going to keep him from his miracle. He refused to give up, and he received his healing.

In Luke 5, a paralyzed man wasn't going to miss receiving his miracle just because it didn't seem possible to get to Jesus. His friends took him "up on the roof and let him down through the tiles with his stretcher, right in the center, in front of Jesus" (v. 19), and he was made whole. Like this overcomer, be tenacious! Refuse to live in the state of hope deferred. Do whatever is necessary to receive your breakthrough.

Expect your heart to get well. Expect the clouds of doubt to yield to the dawn of hope. Expect a new beginning in your life. Expect to enjoy life again. Expect to win.

Expect!

ENDNOTES

Chapter 1

1. Jack Canfield, Mark Victor Hansen and Barry Spilchuk, *A Cup of Chicken Soup for the Soul* (Deerfield Beach FL: Health Communications Inc, 1996), pp. 186-187.
2. Spiros Zodhiates, *Illustrations of Bible Truths* (Chattanooga, TN: AMG Publishers, 1995), p. 5.
3. Marilyn B. Oden, *100 Meditations on Hope* (Nashville, TN: Upper Room Books, 1995), p. 32.
4. While the television broadcast of this movie was edited, I understand the movie itself contains inappropriate language and activities. Thus, I would not want anyone to misconstrue my referring to it as a recommendation of the unedited version of the movie.
5. Craig Brian Larson, *Choice Contemporary Stories and Illustrations* (Grand Rapids MI: Baker Book House, 1998), p. 128.
6. Sue Ellin Browder, "The Heart Quiz That Could Save Your Life," *Reader's Digest* (February 2002), p. 144.
7. *Shiloh Place Ministries*, 2002. http://www.shilohplace.org/crisisin.htm (accessed February 26, 2002).
8. "U.S. Divorce Stats," *DivorceMagazine.com*, 2000. http://www.divorcemag.com/statistics/statsUS.shtml (accessed February 20, 2002).
9. D. L. Hoyert, K. D. Kochanek and S. L. Murphy, "The Numbers Count," *National Institute of Mental Health*, January 2001. http://www.nimh.nih.gov/publicat/numbers.cfm (accessed February 20, 2002).

10. "Depression: On the Edge," *In the Mix Show Stats.* http://www.pbs.org/inthemix/shows/showstats_depression. html (accessed February 20, 2002).

11. "Facts and Figures About Mental Health," *Nation's Voice on Mental Health,* January 2001. http://www.nami.org/fact.htm (accessed February 20, 2002).

12. *Shiloh Place Ministries,* 2002. http://www.shilohplace.org/ crisisin.htm (accessed February 26, 2002).

13. Oden, *100 Meditations on Hope,* p. 11.

14. Craig Brian Larson, *Contemporary Illustrations for Preachers, Teachers, and Writers* (Grand Rapids, MI: Baker Book House, 1996), p. 183.

Chapter 2

1. Marilyn B. Oden, *100 Meditations on Hope* (Nashville, TN: Upper Room Books, 1995), p. 17.

2. James Strong, *The New Strong's Exhaustive Concordance of the Bible* (Nashville, TN: Thomas Nelson Publishers, 1990), s.v. "tiqvah," ref. no. 8615.

3. Ibid., s.v. "qavah," ref. no. 6960.

4. Oden, *100 Meditations on Hope,* p. 25.

5. Robert J. Morgan, *Real Stories for the Soul* (Nashville, TN: Thomas Nelson Publishers, 2000), pp. 53-55.

6. Edward Mote and William Bradbury, "The Solid Rock," *The Celebration Hymnal* (Nashville, TN: Word Music/Integrity Music, 1997), p. 526.

7. Curtis Vaughan, ed., *The Word: The Bible from Twenty-Six Translations* (Atlanta, GA: Mathis Publishers, 1993).

8. *The Great American Bathroom Book,* vol. 1 (Salt Lake City, UT: Compact Classics, Inc., 1991), p. 130.

9. Ibid.

10. Morgan, Real *Stories for the Soul*, pp. 120-121 (emphasis added).

11. Paul Pearsall, *The Ten Laws of Lasting Love* (New York: Simon and Schuster, 1993), n.p. (emphasis added).

12. Craig Brian Larson, *Choice Contemporary Stories and Illustrations for Preachers, Teachers and Writers* (Grand Rapids, MI: Baker Book House, 1998), p. 228.

Chapter 3

1. Jack Canfield, Mark Victor Hansen and Heather McNamara, *Chicken Soup for the Unsinkable Soul* (Deerfield Beach, FL: Health Communications, Inc., 1999), p. 58.

2. Spiros Zodhiates, *The Complete Word Study Dictionary* (Iowa Falls, IA: World Bible Publishers, Inc., 1992), p. 570.

3. Marilyn B. Oden, *100 Meditations on Hope* (Nashville, TN: Upper Room Books, 1995), p. 72.

4. Spiros Zodhiates, *Hebrew-Greek Key Study Bible—New American Standard*, rev. ed. (Chattanooga, TN: AMG Publishers, 1990), p. 1785.

5. Canfield, Hansen and McNamara, *Chicken Soup for the Unsinkable Soul*, pp. 142-143.

6. Ibid., p. 63.

7. "Wilma Rudolph Biography," Women in History, May 2002. http://www.lkwdpl.org/wihohio/rudo-wil.htm (accessed March 5, 2002).

8. Robert J. Morgan, *Real Stories for the Soul* (Nashville, TN: Thomas Nelson Publishers, 2000), pp. 117-119 (emphasis added).

9. Zodhiates, *Hebrew-Greek Key Study Bible—New American Standard*, p. 1716.

10. Ibid., p. 1712.

11. James Strong, *The New Strong's Exhaustive Concordance of the Bible* (Nashville, TN: Thomas Nelson Publishers, 1990), s.v. "nachal," ref. no. 5158.

12. *New Webster's Dictionary and Thesaurus of the English Language,* s.v. "synergism."
13. Edward K. Rowell, *Fresh Illustrations for Preaching and Teaching* (Grand Rapids, MI: Baker Book House, 1997), p. 118.
14. Zodhiates, *Hebrew-Greek Key Study Bible—New American Standard,* p. 1796.
15. Ted Kyle and John Todd, *A Treasury of Bible Illustrations* (Chattanooga, TN: AMG Publishers, 1995), p. 215.

Chapter 4

1. Craig Brian Larson, *Illustrations for Preaching and Teaching* (Grand Rapids, MI: Baker Book House, 1993), p. 91.
2. Rubem Alves, quoted in *Spiritual Literacy: Reading the Sacred in Everyday Life,* comp. Frederic and Mary Ann Brussat (New York: Simon and Schuster, 1996), p. 194.
3. Source unknown.
4. Spiros Zodhiates, *Illustrations of Bible Truths* (Chattanooga, TN: AMG Publishers, 1995), p. 267.
5. Craig Brian Larson, *Contemporary Illustrations for Preachers, Teachers and Writers* (Grand Rapids, MI: Baker Book House, 1996), p. 110.
6. Craig Brian Larson, *Choice Contemporary Stories and Illustrations for Preachers, Teachers and Writers* (Grand Rapids MI: Baker Book House, 1998), p. 20.
7. James Strong, *The New Strong's Exhaustive Concordance of the Bible* (Nashville, TN: Thomas Nelson Publishers, 1990), s.v. "katanoeo," ref. no. 2657.
8. Ibid., s.v. "paroxusmos," ref. no. 3948.
9. Spiros Zodhiates, *Hebrew-Greek Key Study Bible—New American Standard,* rev. ed. (Chattanooga, TN: AMG Publishers, 1990), p. 1864.

10. Larson, *Illustrations for Preaching and Teaching*, p. 144.

Chapter 5
1. Edward K. Rowell, *Fresh Illustrations for Preaching and Teaching* (Grand Rapids, MI: Baker Book House, 1997), p. 148.
2. In order to understand the events associated with Horeb, it is important to note the connection between Mount Horeb and Mount Sinai in the Scriptures. Scholars are unclear whether Sinai was part of a mountain called Horeb, or if Horeb was part of a mountain called Sinai. But historically and contextually they are considered part of the same mountain.
3. Rich DeVos, *Hope From My Heart* (Nashville, TN: Thomas Nelson Publishers, 2000), pp. 27,33.
4. Ethelbert W. Bullinger, *A Critical Lexicon and Concordance to the English and Greek New Testament* (Grand Rapids, MI: Zondervan Publishing House, 1975), p. 804.
5. James Strong, *The New Strong's Exhaustive Concordance of the Bible* (Nashville, TN: Thomas Nelson Publishers, 1990), s.v. "idios," ref. no. 2398.
6. Robert J. Morgan, *Real Stories for the Soul* (Nashville, TN: Thomas Nelson Publishers, 2000), pp. 158-159.
7. Strong, *The New Strong's Exhaustive Concordance of the Bible*, s.v. "abar," ref. no. 5674.
8. Spiros Zodhiates, *Hebrew-Greek Key Study Bible—New American Standard*, rev. ed. (Chattanooga, TN: AMG Publishers, 1990), p. 1756.
9. Ibid.
10. Bobbye Byerly, *Miracles Happen When Women Pray* (Ventura, CA: Regal Books, 2002), pp. 40-45.

Chapter 6

1. Alice Gray, *More Stories for the Heart* (Sisters, OR: Multnomah Publishers, Inc., 1997), p. 247.

2. James Strong, *The New Strong's Exhaustive Concordance of the Bible* (Nashville, TN: Thomas Nelson Publishers, 1990), s.v. "matteh," ref. no. 4294

3. Neil T. Anderson, *Victory over the Darkness* (Ventura, CA: Regal Books, 1990), pp. 87-88.

4. Sandy Dengler, *Susanna Wesley, Servant of God* (Chicago, IL: Moody Press, 1987), n.p.

5. Catherine Marshall, "Timeless Treasures," *Spirit Led Woman* (February/March 2002), pp. 66-67.

6. Gray, *More Stories for the Heart*, p. 220.

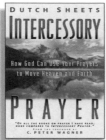
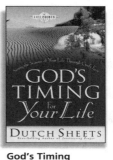

PRAY WITH POWER

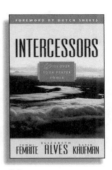

ecoming a Prayer Warrior
Guide to Effective and Powerful
ayer
zabeth Alves
perback • ISBN 08307.23331

Beyond the Veil
Entering into Intimacy
with God Through Prayer
Alice Smith
Paperback • ISBN 08307.20707

Intercessors
Discover Your Prayer Anointing
Tommi Femrite, Elizabeth Alves
& Karen Kaufman
Paperback • ISBN 08307.26446

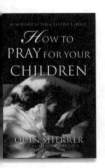

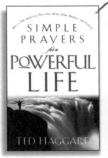

**How to Pray for
Your Children**
Gain Hope and Guidance in
Praying for Your Children
Quin Sherrer
Paperback • ISBN 08307.22017
Video • UPC 607135.003878

**Simple Prayers
for a Powerful Life**
How to Take Authority over
Your Mind, Home, Business
and Country
Ted Haggard
Paperback • ISBN 08307.30559

**Praying the Bible:
The Book of Prayers**
Praying God's Word Out Loud
for Spiritual Breakthrough
Wesley and Stacey Campbell
Paperback • ISBN
08307.30672